THE COLLECTOR
OF LEFTOVER
SOULS

THE COLLECTOR OF LEFTOVER SOULS

Dispatches from Brazil

Eliane Brum

Translated from the Portuguese by Diane Grosklaus Whitty

GRANTA

Granta Publications, 12 Addison Avenue, London W11 4QR

First published in Great Britain by Granta Books, 2019
Originally published in the United States in 2019 by Graywolf Press, Minneapolis,
Minnesota

Published with the support of the Ministry of Citizenship of Brazil | National Library
Foundation. Obra publicada com o apoio do Ministério da Cidadania do Brasil |
Fundação Biblioteca Nacional.

A CIP catalogue record for this book is available from the British Library.
1 3 5 7 9 10 8 6 4 2

ISBN 978 1 84627 664 4
eISBN 978 1 84627 666 8

Book design by Rachel Holscher
Set in Adobe Garamond Pro by Bookmobile Design and Digital Publisher Services,
Minneapolis, Minnesota
Offset by AvonDataSet Ltd, Bidford on Avon, Warwickshire, B50 4JH

Printed and bound by CPI Group (UK) Ltd, Croydon, CR0 4YY

www.granta.com

*For Maíra, who grew into a woman,
living with me between Brazils*

CONTENTS

THE COLLECTOR
OF LEFTOVER
SOULS

INTRODUCTION: BETWEEN WORLDS

Being a journalist, or being the journalist I am, means putting on the skin of the Other. And the Other's skin is language, the first world we each inhabit. Everyone who lives in the words of this book lives in the Brazilian language, in the Portuguese that came along with the colonizers but was invaded by the tongues of the indigenous peoples who were already living here, in Brazil's before, and by the tongues of the various African peoples who reached this land enslaved. Among the many ways they rose up was to contaminate the masters' vowels and consonants. They infected the body's language, placing curves where the Portuguese colonizers had threatened right angles, acute and cutting. They made music where earlier the whip had cracked. What I call the Brazilian language—or Brazilian Portuguese—is a language of insurrections. My language and that of all the inhabitants of these pages.

These real stories told in an insubordinate tongue have for the first time been rendered in English. That this encounter will not be an act of violence but of possibility is the dream contained within this book. Its publication comes at a time when part of the world is

3

endeavoring to build ever higher walls to keep insurgent languages from invading those who deem themselves pure, those who fear contagion from other experiences in being. In this sense, this book, which carries the insurrections of my language into English, is also what books should be, a sledgehammer for demolishing barriers. If you have opened it, this book by a Brazilian journalist, it is because you don't like walls either.

Whenever I visit an English-speaking country, I notice Brazil doesn't exist for most of you. Or exists only in the stereotype of Carnival and soccer. Favelas, butts, and violence. Lots of corruption, in recent years. In the first decade of this century, Brazil sparked global interest when Luiz Inácio Lula da Silva, a metalworker who became president, performed a bit of magic, reducing poverty without touching the privileges of the wealthiest. What is called the First World really liked this magic, because it blurred the inequality explicit in the geopolitics of our planet, an inequity with deep historical roots. And it also made everyone happy without anybody having to lose anything in order to achieve a minimum level of social justice. As the following years proved, there is no magic. Since Brazil couldn't perform magic, it returned to its place in the background of the "wealthy" world's imagination. Nobody gets popular by saying wealth has to be distributed so that the expendables will stop dying from hunger and bullets.

And then, in 2018, Brazil returned to the world spotlight because it elected Jair Bolsonaro, a man who defends torture and torturers; insults black people, women, and gays; and declares that minorities must vanish and that his opponents are destined for exile or jail. At the close of the 2010s, Brazil thus joined the ranks of countries that committed the contradictory act of voting down democracy by electing a defender of dictatorship. Once again, that which is unique or singular must resist between the lines, and small everyday insurrections are what make life hold steadfast in the face of a culture of death.

Brazil is a country that exists only in the plural. The Brazils. In the singular, it's an impossibility. Since we are the Brazils, and not Brazil, there are also many Brazilian tongues. My challenge as a reporter is reaching these diverse tongues and converting them into written words without reducing them or the world of their telling. This is a challenge I fail at while trying.

The Brazils hold the largest part of the world's largest tropical forest, strategic wealth in a world haunted by human-made climate change. The forest is a power at this moment when humans have quit fearing catastrophe to become the catastrophe they feared. Since 1998, I have been roaming the Amazons, listening to the stories of peoples, trees, and animals. As I write this introduction, I have been living in Altamira, a city in the Amazon forest, on the banks of the Xingu River, for a year.

This book begins with a birth in the forest and ends with a death on the periphery of Greater São Paulo, the largest urban conglomeration in Brazil and one of the world's ten largest. At more than twenty million, its population surpasses that of countries like Portugal and the Netherlands. When I'm not in the Amazons, I'm in this desert of buildings where rivers are interred and covered by concrete tombs, over which we walk, always in a rush. I make my body a bridge between such diverse Brazils.

The Collector of Leftover Souls: Field Notes on Brazil's Everyday Insurrections brings together stories from two distinct moments in my life as a reporter. The shorter feature reports were written in 1999. I was working that year at *Zero Hora*, a newspaper in far southern Brazil, the region where I was born. Every Saturday, I had a column called "The Life No One Sees." In this one-page space, I wrote stories about what we usually define as "ordinary people." Those who don't make the news in the paper. Or whose lives—and deaths—are reduced to a footnote so tiny it almost slides off the page. I wrote precisely to show there are no ordinary lives, only domesticated eyes. Eyes incapable of seeing that every life is spun from the thread of the extraordinary.

Resisting the domestication of our eyes by reaching for the singularity of each person's life is what allowed me to stitch each small report together. The political content of these "unhappenings"—a word I invented to convey the journalism I do—is that no one is replaceable. So the lives of some cannot be worth more than the lives of others. Years later, this collection of stories became a book, and this book was awarded Brazil's top literary prize in the journalism category.

The eight short reports chosen for inclusion in the present book express what drives me as a journalist. How each person invents a life, naked and with so little, is what fascinates me. This is also what carries me through so many worlds and so many languages. I want to learn from these stubborn people how they lend meaning to what has none and create a human existence. Our life is our first fiction. This fiction, which we call reality, is the substance of my stories.

Short reports, much investigating. I believe in news stories as documents of everyday history, as life told, as witness. I practice journalism with rigor, seeking precision and respecting the exact word. But also with the conviction that reality is an intricate fabric, sewn not only from words but also from textures, smells, colors, gestures. Marks. From voids, excesses, nuances, and silences. Ruins.

My personal conception of reportage was constructed over the last thirty years, in which nearly every day of my life was devoted to reaching a world foreign to me—and a world that thought I was foreign. A news story is not only found out on the street, by getting your shoes dirty, as so often said. A news story also demands an initial radical movement: crossing the wide street of yourself. This is perhaps the most profound and also the hardest act. It demands that you uninhabit yourself to inhabit the Other, the world that is the Other. We become capable of accomplishing this only by listening with all of our senses, the kind of listening that palpates what is said as much as what goes unsaid, what sounds and resounds as much as what is silent. The texture of furniture as much as the choice of pictures on a wall. Smells and absences. Denials, frights, and hesitations. The incompleteness of bitten fingernails, the polish chosen or forgotten. The gaps. And the leftovers.

A news story means stripping off the clothes of ourselves to don the Other. Stripping ourselves of biases, judgments, worldviews, in order to don another experience in being and existing on this planet. And then undertaking the long path back and giving birth to the words, which is the story told, crossed by the body of the one who has returned to share news from there. From a there that through the movement of the story becomes there and here.

It is through this gesture that I also reach those for whom the word is not written. As a reporter, I have often found myself before illiterates who produce literature with their mouths. They have made me who I am, as much as the celebrated writers I've met on library shelves. Men and women who rest their hoes against a rock or lay their fishing rods down in the canoe to tell of their lives in a poetic prose born from a unique experience of the world. They tell their story generously, not realizing they create universes as they tell it. All of these people, now a multitude after thirty years, inhabit and infect me. There's no asepsis in a real encounter with the Other.

Seven of the nine longer feature stories in the present book were written in the first decade of this century, when I was working for a weekly newsmagazine called *Época*, in São Paulo, from 2000 to 2008. They are part of another book, entitled *Olho da Rua—uma repórter em busca da literatura da vida real* (Eye of the street: a reporter in search of the literature of real life). Many of these essays show what is nonnegotiable in the journalism I practice. In "Forest of Midwives," I try to leave clear my absolute conviction, woven from experience, that listening is the main tool in reportage.

As a reporter (and as a person), I've always thought that more important than knowing how to ask a question is knowing how to listen to the answer. When possible, I don't even ask the first question. I think the first question says more about me than about the person I want to reach. The first question also hints to the interviewee about the reporter's wishes. The first question is a form of control. And to be a good listener, I need to relinquish control. So I just say: "Tell me . . . " And it's surprising where people begin telling their story.

The richness of the midwives' language and the way each of them expressed herself is the heart of the first chapter. They spoke with such beauty, with such amazing variety and profundity, that my work was minimal. It sufficed just to listen and write down every sigh to miss nothing. Not even if I'd wanted to, not even if I were writing fiction and had permission to make things up, would I have come close to the beauty with which they spoke. Especially in this story, my work as a reporter was to listen to each gesture, emphasis, facial expression, and put it all down on paper. It was almost like channeling living persons.

It's only a joy to be a reporter when we surrender to the story and let it turn us inside out. If I ever come back the same from a trip to the forest of Amapá or the periphery of São Paulo, I'll give up journalism. Being a reporter is being reborn and re-creating oneself with each story. Preferably, through natural childbirth.

If you're a reader who reads as if you're listening to music, you'll notice that each story in *The Collector of Leftover Souls* has its own words, rhythms, and arrangements. If this were not the case, something fateful would have happened to me. I would have traversed the Brazils, and the Brazils inside each Brazil, but I would not really have left my own house. Without recognizing the Other's language and the rhythm at which life is told within each different geography, I would be condemned to write only about myself and my restricted universe of language. Even if there were other names and supposedly other stories, I'd be the author of one single news report, with the same character: me.

For "Old Folks Home," I spent a week living in an institution that houses people from all social classes, reproducing inside the inequality from the outside. And I was soon overcome by the weight of those walls. I immediately felt cut off from the outer world. I adapt easily to the places I go—be it a tent in a mining region, a lean-to in a favela, or a room in a nursing home. I like knowing I have a home to return to, but I feel profoundly in my place out of place. And when I return, I have trouble adapting because of the intensity with which I surrendered. When I get home, I feel my body has been elongated, stretched between two worlds. I have one foot left there, an elbow, sometimes an eye. I have to pull myself back slowly, sometimes by the hair.

For me, writing is a physical, carnal act. Those who know me know the literalness of how I live. And primarily the literalness of how I write. I am what I write. This is not a rhetorical image. I feel as if every word, written inside my body with blood, fluids, and nerves, were really made of blood, fluids, and nerves. When the text becomes written word, a code on the computer screen, it is still my flesh. I feel physical pain, real and concrete, during this birth. I am overtaken by this experience.

Sometimes people ask me: Do you get involved with your sources? Of course I do. We don't enter someone else's life with impunity. Sometimes I feel too insufficient. I know that no life fits completely into words. But some experiences are even more rebellious, refusing to become subject, verb, and predicate. They escape, slip away into language without converting into writing. This is what happened in "The Middle People." I was the first journalist to reach the Amazon

forest community whose story is told in this chapter. I was immediately overcome by angst. How could I witness the struggle of a
handful of forgotten Brazilians, invisible and so fragile, living well
beyond the (readers') ends of the earth, and tell this in a few para-
graphs or pages?

The journey to Middle Land was one of those moments that can't
be reduced to writing. Just like my love for the Amazon, which is
well beyond any destination anywhere in the world, and my gratitude for the assignment that led me to this region, an improbable
place even for the Amazon. When this happens, this inability to
transform what is lived into writing, all that is left us is to humbly
accept these limits. And to feel a secret joy over the privilege of living something that can't be said.

My report, so insufficient given the size of the reality, was deci-
sive in stopping the Middle People from dying by bullet. After the
story, the leaders—Herculano, Raimundo, and Manchinha—were
fished out of the forest, put on a plane, and taken to the official
Brazil, that of Brasilia, to tell ministers of state what they were living through. They came to exist for the other Brazils. Little River
became an extractive reserve protected by federal law. And today
I am spoken of in the history that the elders verbally pass down to
the younger ones. We have grown old together, I and they, and we
have witnessed the youth who have begun fighting for the forest
with which they merge. This is one of those moments when the joy
of being a reporter doesn't fit into words. It is worth a life.

I believe the best news stories are the result of an assignment
that got complicated. If a colleague asks me for advice, I begin by
saying, "Complicate your assignment." The idea that comes easily
is always the most obvious, the one that's in your head because it
was already somewhere else before. For years, I had tried to convince various bosses of mine that journalism had the ethical obliga-
tion to show it can't be "normal" for a generation of Brazilian youth,

most of them black, to have a life expectancy of twenty. But since newsrooms had been overrun in recent decades by middle-class journalists, most of them white, it was hard to convince them. These journalists grew up and became adults in a country where the death of young black people is a daily unhappening as "natural" as a traffic jam in São Paulo.

I was able to start my report on "Living Mothers of a Dead Generation" only when I complicated my assignment. There was something that ran through the tension between races and social classes, something I had fought on other fronts but that could form a bridge between worlds: the myth of motherhood. So I decided to tell of the children's deaths through their mothers' pain. The pain for which, yet again, there is no word in my language. Nor in yours. The mother who loses a child is not an orphan, not a widow. This pain has been left out of language.

When I went to live for a time in Brasilândia, a neighborhood on the periphery of São Paulo, I had a different quest. If there were nothing but violence and death in Brazil's favelas, one would expect an epidemic of suicides. But that's not the case. On the contrary, there is almost a stubbornness not only to live but to live with joy. Joy, I was to learn over the years, is the greatest act of resistance in a human's life.

I disembarked in Brasilândia to investigate the delicate things that made life possible, even in brutal hours. So I spent the first two days just observing the new world, letting Tuca and Dona Eugênia, my hostesses, take me here and there, and making myself almost as expressive as a head of kale, deflating their expectations about the "journalist" who had landed there. This was the only way I could capture the poignant beauty of the collective effort behind Adriana and Luiz's wedding.

My challenge was to remain a foreigner in order to maintain an eye of astonishment, essential to seeing a layer beyond the obvious.

But I had to do so without allowing myself to be contaminated by a tourist's eye, which sees reality filtered through biases or fantasies. Tourists see only what they expect to, what they believe to be true about that reality—and for that, you don't need to leave home.

A journalist is an intimate foreigner. Whenever I go into the Other's universe, I need to understand something crucial: When someone introduces me to her world, what does she show me and what doesn't she? What paths does she lead me on? What words does she use to name her territory, the one inside and the one outside? And why? The favela, as I would learn, was always located a little farther on. I would ask: "Where does the favela begin?" And the person would point about a hundred yards ahead. I'd walk over there and ask the person outside his home: "Is this the favela here?" It never was. The favela was—always—one hundred yards farther along.

In "In Demon Zé's Brazil," I tell of the birth of a gold mining region in the heart of the forest. I stick my feet in the mud of human passions to show who these men and women so filled with desires are. Only the hookers arrive at the gold pit before the prospectors. Or they arrive together. The prospector, seen as coarse, as a thug and a destroyer of the forest, is the poor Brazilian who refuses to give up. Described as ugly, dirty, and mean, he defies the logic of capital, the logic that sells big mining concerns, usually transnational corporations, as "entrepreneurs," "clean," and "legal." In his yearning for a place in the Brazils, the prospector propels his body into the oldest conflict in the world. The delicacy and the many dreams of this harsh world are also what I am looking for, beyond the labels that box people up.

The book closes with the end of a life. For 115 days, I accompanied the day-to-day of a woman with incurable cancer. The first time I saw her, Ailce de Oliveira Souza was in the middle of her living room, a poorly disguised look of expectation on her face. I was a journalist who would tell her story to the end, but at that moment she was pretending she didn't know the end would be death. Like every one of us, upon getting out of bed in the morning, many times she too believed fiercely that she wouldn't die.

Who was I? At that moment, March 26, 2008, I was a reporter who didn't know what she was doing. I had decided to follow someone with an incurable disease to the end. But I didn't have any measure of the abyssal consequences of this choice. The instant our eyes met in the silence of Ailce's living room, I put myself in an impossible situation: my life tied itself to her death.

I could never want this assignment to be over. And at the same time, I wanted it to be over as quickly as possible. I grew more and more anxious to free myself from such everyday contact with dying that it was making my life impossible. At the same time, I pretended my newsgathering would never be over. In a way, she and I were two pretenders. Her, in the position of a character from a life, me as the narrator of a story whose end was the end of her life.

With the publication of the story, I fulfilled my part of the pact. Her part was allowing me to witness her dying. Mine was to reconstitute her body with words, make it alive through writing. Only then did I realize that no one else had ever trusted me so much: I would write a story she would never read.

Some people have asked me about a reporter's level of intervention, me, intersecting with the character, her. This is a topic dear to the practice of journalism. For journalists, impartiality and objectivity stand as ideals that must be pursued but will never be fully realized. Our mere presence—or the decision to write a story—in itself alters the reality about which we will write. The clearer this is for the reader, the more honest our work.

I've never seen myself in the position of a god who observes a given reality from the outside, immune to its implications. I am well aware of the weaknesses of my humanity and I see myself as the cultural expression of a certain historical era, much less free than I would like to be. In my texts, I try to make it very clear to the reader what my place is and where my interference altered the narrative.

During the 115 days that Ailce and I shared our lives—a radical experience in journalism but especially a radical experience in life—I devoted obsessive care to avoiding any interference in her lived experience of dying. I hardly asked any questions. I opted merely to underscore her answers, through delicate and very, very attentive listening. On the one hand, my questions, if trenchant, would contaminate her answers: she might use my words instead of hers to refer to this extreme moment of life. On the other, I would risk infringing on her sensibility if I ventured questions she wasn't ready for yet.

In the first case, such interference would make honest reportage impossible. In the second, it would hurt Ailce. One example: she never used the word *cancer*, and I never pronounced the word *cancer*. If I had said *cancer*, I couldn't have known that Ailce didn't use this word, and therefore I wouldn't understand something crucial about how she coped with the disease that would kill her. I never talked about "death" before her. If I had rashly set about asking, I wouldn't have known how much time Ailce needed to utter the word *death*. Nor all the implications of this noisy silence. Nor would I know she only talked about life. In this story, these are the interventions that, if consummated, would condemn the narrative of Ailce's life. But would I drip water into her mouth when she no longer had the strength to hold a glass, or help her bathe when there was no one else to do it? Yes. These acts don't have anything to do with journalism. Only with humanity.

The two other pieces in this book are feature stories on topics to which I devoted many years of my life as a reporter. "The Noise" has followed me since the first time I listened to a worker contaminated by asbestos, air being laboriously sucked in by a lung turning to stone. I listened to his words, but what I listened to more was the awful sound he made to keep himself alive. As long as I myself live, this noise will breathe on as a memory in my brain. The essay published here tells the story of one out of dozens of workers whom I have followed over the first two decades of this century. Men and women in search of air, justice, and the banning of asbestos in Brazil and the world. The story says more of me, listening to it.

After so many news stories over so many years, I could no longer stand the horror of witnessing their deaths without justice, of still hearing CEOs and lobbyists affirm that this carcinogenic fiber is safe, of continuing to watch as a billionaire who grew rich from asbestos cleansed his biography, converting himself into an environmentalist, a Maecenas, and a "good man" recognized around the world. So I wrote this essay for a book entitled *O verso dos trabalhadores* (Workers' verse), a collection by various authors, published in 2015. I made this noise my noise, hoping more people could listen to it when it also became word.

After thirty years of reporting, I am haunted by the dead whose lives could not be changed through any denunciation of mine. I keep trying to discover the words with which I can tell their stories so they will be listened to, how I can find a place for these buried yet unburied voices, so they can become memory. "The Noise" is part of this effort. It took me a while to understand that what's missing are not words or voices. What's missing are ears.

Since 2011, I have followed those affected by Belo Monte, Beautiful Mountain, designed to be one of the world's largest hydroelectric power plants. Those who have been reached by its steel and concrete arm call it the "monster." *Belo Monstro*, Beautiful Monster. Through their eyes and also mine, I saw the monster rise up on the Xingu, one of the grandest rivers in the Amazon, killing water and life. Belo Monte is not just one more public works project imposed on the forest and its people. It is the serpent's egg where today's Brazil was designed.

"João Asks Raimunda to Die with Him in Sacrifice" tells of this monstrous gestation. And of how it produced what I have called refugees within their own country. This is the point in my life where I am today. My country is a big builder of ruins. Brazil builds ruins of continental dimensions. Tucked away in the Amazon forest, I tell how men and women who have been reduced to the territory of their own bodies invent a life after death.

I don't know much about myself. When I think I know a little, I do my own unmasking and slip away from myself. My only certainty, perhaps, is that I'm a reporter. Inhabiting bodies, converting this experience into words, is something visceral, definitive of what I am. All of how I view the world is mediated by an incommensurate love for the infinite absurdity of reality. With the Guarani-Kaiowá, an indigenous people murdered in many ways for centuries and who resist nonetheless, I learned another word: *ñe'ẽ*. It is word and soul at the same time. It is in this other language, neither mine nor yours, that I find something that defines my search. In the vortex of the between-worlds, I want to be a word that acts.

In this book, as in life, all I have to offer is myself. I hope that is sufficient.

Altamira, Brazil, November 14, 2018

FOREST OF MIDWIVES

They were born from the humid womb of the Amazon, in a state called Amapá in far northern Brazil, still adrift from the news. The country doesn't hear them because it has lost its ear for the sounds of ancient knowledge, for the cadence of their melodies. Many of them don't know the letters of the alphabet, but they read the forest, the water, and the sky. They emerged from the realms of other women who had the gift of catching babies. Theirs is a wisdom that can't be learned, or taught, or even explained. It just happens. Their hands, furrowed by the blood of women and the water of children, receive a piece of Brazil.

An atavistic, female cry echoes from this land, poised at the peak of the map, reminding the country that birth is natural. It doesn't depend on genetic engineering or surgery and doesn't smell like a hospital. For the midwives of the forest, who have safeguarded this tradition thanks to the geographical isolation of their birthplace, it is easier to understand that a dolphin can rise out of a stream to impregnate a young maiden than to accept the idea that a woman schedules the time and day to have her child pulled out by force.

Amapá has fewer than half a million inhabitants, and most of them made their debut into the world through the hands of seven hundred baby catchers. These are women who conjugate their verbs in the plural, who wear out collective pronouns. In the logic of their lives, "I" is an outsider who enjoys no special privileges.

Perched in a boat or feeling out paths with their feet, there go the Indian Dorica, the brown *cabocla* Jovelina, the black *quilombola* Rossilda. They are guides on a journey through mysteries that have been passed down from generation to generation, with words that were inscribed in the world without ever being transcribed. Their paths meet with the paths of Tereza and other indigenous midwives of Oiapoque, united, all of them, by the web of births documented in the marks on the palms of their hands.

"Catching babies means being patient," says the Karipuna Indian Maria dos Santos Maciel, Dorica, at ninety-six Amapá's oldest midwife. More than two thousand Indians have disembarked in the world through her tiny, almost childlike hands. Dorica—grandmother, mother, godmother to hundreds of caught children—actually doesn't like having the gift. "The gift's like that, born with us. And you can't say no." Dorica, the indigenous midwife, stretches the colonizer's language, poetizing the awesome: "A midwife has no choice, she's called in the dead hours of the night to people the world."

Like a female apparition, Dorica navigates the tributaries of the Oiapoque, illuminated only by an oil lamp. She travels in the company of her sixty-six-year-old sister, Alexandrina, nine of whose eleven children she has helped birth. "Woman and forest are one and the same," says Alexandrina. "Mother Earth has everything, just like everything is found in a woman's body. Strength, courage, life, pleasure."

When their oars slice through the silent river, they are pursued by the firefly eyes of caimans. "There's no danger. Caimans only eat dogs and sandals," Dorica says. "We opened one up a little while ago and that was all there was." She remembers her own belly's sixteen miscarriages, preventing her from bearing her own child by designs not hers to question. "I'm tired," she announces. "I'd like to ask God for my retirement from midwifery."

God is even more leisurely than the minister of social security. So far he hasn't replied to her request. So Dorica still digs her bare feet into the ground whenever she reaches her destination and crouches down between the woman's thighs. Alexandrina sits behind the mother-to-be, hugging the woman with her own legs. Dorica never yanks anything from the inner recesses of the female body; she just waits. She presses and pulls the mother's belly, righting the child. She smears oil of tapir, ray, or opossum on her tummy and recites prayers and incantations to consummate the mystery. She ruptures the woman's waters with her fingernail and cuts the umbilical cord with an arrowhead, or with her teeth. "Catching babies is about waiting for the time to be born," she teaches. "The doctors in the city don't know how, and since they don't, they cut the woman open."

Dorica abandons her manioc field for eight days. For the midwife, it is her mission to wash, cook, and pull the woman's belly every morning and every afternoon so she will be healthy. It is her duty to pass a fine-tooth comb and water from a white gourd over the woman's breasts so her milk will gush between the baby's lips. It is wise to aspirate the baby's nose with her own mouth until she hears its cry. When this period ends, Dorica hands the woman over to her husband: "I've done what I can for her. Now you've got to take care of your family." The husband thanks her: "If I can give you something, I will." Dorica replies: "God pays it back." The conversation is over. That's all. And it's been like this for well over five hundred years.

The woman will open the door of her home only forty days later, together with her child. Before breathing the forest air, the baby is blessed with water and salt to ward off evil spirits. Out of more than two thousand births, Dorica has lost only three babies. A day doesn't go by when she doesn't mourn them: "It's a child missing from the community." As the peoples of the forest understand things, nobody is replaceable. Or disposable. The life that withered before it took root is unique.

The midwife bids farewell as our canoe vanishes down the river. A macaw watches her from a branch, a flock of shrieking parrots cuts through the sky, a young girl bathes in the waters of a stream, getting ready for school. It's an ordinary day. Dorica rests her hand on her old heart and, mouthing silent words, draws from there the blessing for those who depart. Then she turns her back and goes off to puff tobacco while she waits for the hour when the fifth child of the village's latest mother-to-be, the Indian Ivaneide Iapará, will pound on the gateway to the world, announcing that he is coming on through.

Today most of the midwives of the forest observe the Catholic religion, while some have embraced born-again faiths. Still others practice Spiritism or Candomblé. Whether they invoke a male Christian god, the Holy Spirit, or *orixás*, they proclaim themselves guardians of a mystery handed down by their mothers and grandmothers, a chain that has gotten lost in the centuries. Within this nameless spirituality, they say the great deity is female, a woman. She is the one, they affirm, who rules the beginning-middle-end, birth-life-death, and present-past-future.

When they row down rivers for miles or travel on foot to help a peer achieve the miracle, childbirth is resistance and subversion, proof that every woman has a bit of the goddess in her. Many midwives were burned by the Inquisition. These women, who still heed the call today, did not learn this in history books. But in a way, they harbor the heat of those flames in their bones.

At seventy-seven, Jovelina Costa dos Santos is the most famous midwife in Ponta Grossa do Piriri, a village scattered across a few dozen houses and fields, sixty miles from Macapá. "God gave me this distinction," she says from the door. Jovelina has more wrinkles on her face than the night has stars. Cheerful as can be, when she opens her mouth it seems as if a piece of the earth will fall free. It's not that she's happy. She simply laughs because she's decided not to be sad. That's Jovelina, complex simplicity. When she wakes, she doesn't always know if she'll eat before the next break of day. As she sees it, she is richer than most. "Children are riches, my sister, a beautiful thing to see."

More of her philosophy: "Out here in these backwaters of death, either we fill the world with children or we vanish." That is the only way to understand it when the *cabocla* Jovelina hides her teeth, threatening to cast the planet into darkness, and says, "I had only eight." Only? "Only, of course. Giving birth is so good . . ." And she adds with a devilish grin, "I like making them even more."

She made her debut in the craft when she was still a girl, a trap set by God to send her off to her fate. People gather as she tells her tale, which is worth a ticket. "The first was Isabel, Sevério's wife. He was off in Volta das Cobras. 'Don't worry, *compadre*,' mother says, 'Isabel can stay with us.' Isabel got the fever at night, the chills, but she didn't let out a peep. Mother headed to the fields in the morning, me and Isabel stayed. 'Jovita, Jovita, get the bath water ready.'" She interrupts in another tone to explain that Jovita was her. "'Here it is, Isabel,' I say. 'You know, before dawn I got some horrific chills,' she says. 'You did, Isabel?' I say. 'I did, Jovita.' I was combing my hair when it spilled out. 'Jovita, little sister, help me.' Isabel got under the mosquito netting and I caught the baby. He was cold, dead. When mother got back, she asked me, 'How did it go, Jovita?' 'All right, mother.' Then she said, 'Well, daughter, from now on you'll go in my place.' And I did."

Jovelina counts only on Saint Bartholomew as her helper, the patron of midwives, like Saint Raymond Nonnatus, Our Lady of Good Birth, and other, more eminent Holinesses. But he's not "Saint Bartholomew." For Jovita, he's "Saint Bartelemee," a bit Frenchified and with much more sparkle. "At four in the afternoon, Bartelemee got up and grabbed hold of his staff. Down his path he went. Our Lady he met. She asked, 'Where're you going, Bartelemee?' 'I'm going to Our Lady's house.' 'Go, Bartelemee, and there I'll give you talents. Where women don't die of childbirth, nor do babies smother.'" That's all. Just recite this prayer and the baby slides down into the forest, landing right in the midwife's hands.

The *cabocla* Jovelina has only two shadows in her life. When speaking of them, she even allows herself the luxury of a sigh. One is her first husband, for whom she still carries a torch that blazes inside her, even though he has passed away. "I was crazy about him. But I dumped him. He had me and three other women. Ugh!" The other shadow is doctors, whose ignorance is extraordinary, according to Jovelina. "What these women go through at the hospital is a violence, my friend," she says in horror. "Here, if the baby settles in wrong, we go and turn him. I put my hand there, and pull and pull until he's put right, until he gets his head in place. Then you don't need to cut. Doctors, poor things, don't know how to turn babies."

When it is time for goodbyes, she calls her "belly-button children" to show them off to the visitors. The whole village doesn't appear, but only because a good number are at a soccer tournament in the neighboring district, where both teams came onto the field by way of Jovelina's hands. The midwife plants her crooked Garrincha legs on the doorstep, puts her blessing hands on her waist, and bellows out, "Come here, you band of rascals! Oh, if my mother had sent me to school, I wouldn't have such a hard time." She breaks into another grin to shine up the sky and grows tender: "Bunch of fine-looking kids, aren't they?"

Childbirth is a woman's mystery, done by women, among women; their affair. The midwives of the forest cannot fathom how life unfolds in the cradle of death, in a hospital, as if birth were a disease. In the mind of every midwife, pain heralds the ecstasy of birth, opposites as inseparable as night and day. Childbirth isn't suffering. It's a celebration. "I'm from the days when you had to have mothered a child to know the mystery. Virgin girls didn't talk about sex, so they wouldn't feel pleasure in speaking of it," says sixty-three-year-old Rossilda Joaquina da Silva, eleven children, twenty grandchildren, and four great-grandchildren. "When it's time for the baby to arrive, the women gather and it's a glory."

Rossilda is black, coal black, like the land of the Curiaú quilombo, a former settlement of runaway slaves in the vicinity of Macapá. She spreads her chubby arms, brawny from catching babies, sewing dresses by hand, and blessing the ill. "Inner Curiaú, Outer Curiaú, I've done births over here and over there. They were all born through my hands." Rossilda is solemn like that. She drops her broom to tell her destiny, swaying in her rocking chair to the sound of a melody meant to hasten an entangled birth. "Give me strength, oh Lord, my glorious Saint John. Saint John was anchored in the River Jordan. Help me, O Lord, God of Mercy, the ropes that hear me shall bear me up."

Rossilda's quilombo of Curiaú was celebrating Saint Lazarus, saint of dogs. Because, as Rossilda explains, even dogs have saints. With her habitual gentility, Rossilda tells how lovely the banquet of the dogs was. "They ate beef, Christian food. Each one had his own dish at the table, in a show of respect, courtesy. All very civilized."

Written by the midwife's oldest son, Sabá, the headline in the local paper, *Jornal do Quilombo*, read: "After delivering several head butts, the ram Chibé became a Christmas barbecue." The explanation came on the last page: "Chibé was a very mischievous ram, frisky and brazen. He never missed a chance to chase people around and knock children to the ground. Though everybody misses him, his fate was sealed: he ended up as the Christmas meal."

That is Curiaú, a land fattened by rhymes, from the days when you had to sing on the tree trunk to keep from succumbing to hopelessness. Like her land, Rossilda is a woman steeped in enchantments. Another midwife, Angelina, accompanies her to every birth. Angelina is invoked in spirit, because she left her flesh long ago. Rossilda won't share the secret of this duo, living and non-living: "Otherwise it would lose its worthfulness."

After nine moons have passed, the men of Curiaú are sent on their way so they won't make a mess of things. Because at this point, men only know how to cause a fuss. Childbirth is a women's gathering. Neighbors come from all corners, midwives or not. They crowd into the house, make coffee and porridge, commence telling tales and jokes to distract the mother-to-be. Laughing a little, praying another little, dressed in white from head to toe, Rossilda goes about putting the baby right, watchful of the pain. Before you know it, "there comes the baby sliding into the world." Only then is the father called to cock his rifle and shoot into the air, three times if it's a boy or twice if it happens to be a girl. If it's a boy, it might be yet another Joaquim or Raimundo. If a girl, usually Maria.

That's how Rossilda's children were born: Sebastião, Eraldo, Leonice, Leonilza, Leonira, Leoneide, Lourença, Leicione, Leodenice, Leodivaldo . . . "Did I leave anyone out? Oh yeah, Lucivaldo." It's also how her grandchildren and great-grandchildren were born. And how her great-great-grandchildren will be born. Framed by the doorway and crowned by a cross made of acapu wood, to crush the force of evil, Rossilda bids a rhyming farewell: "I'm a midwife, clean of hands, pure of heart. Birthing babies is my art."

The women's forest is a land of singing. "They said that we were nothing, but oh how they were wrong. Look how we are organized, as midwives we stand strong," chants Tereza Bordalo in the drawling voice of northern Brazil. Age fifty-one, mother to five, grandmother to another five, midwife since the age of sixteen. As she traces out an invisible cross over the woman's vagina, a caiman tooth swings perilously between her profane Madonna breasts.

Later, Tereza prays and performs a secret she won't share with a living soul. A secret that emerged in the middle of the night, in the form of a woman wearing a dress with a long train, the color of the sky. In a whispered voice, she who was not of this world ordered Tereza to get rid of her husband, an innocent guy snoring away on the pillow beside her. Tereza spent night after night in shadowed dreams. She would barely nod off and the lady would appear, formed wholly of dream matter. Weary of fighting with the hereafter, Tereza told João Bordalo to go sleep someplace else. Only then did the spirit reveal why she was there, before vanishing for good. But first she threatened: "Do not reveal my secret to anyone, or I will destroy your power." Tereza has never again run into trouble between a woman's thighs.

Swinging her umbrella, inseparable from her in the Amazon winter, Tereza summons the midwives of the forest for their ritual of thanksgiving. She sets foot in a land teeming with juices, Saint-Georges-de-l'Oyapock, in French Guiana, separated from Brazil and the Oiapoque only by the river of the same name. She greets her friends with a "*Bon soir, ça va bien?*" On the other side of the border, the midwives are all called Madam. Or rather, *Madame.* Like Madame Marie Labonté, a Karipuna with the demeanor of a young girl, who steals into the bush in search of skins left behind by snakes. "If you drink snakeskin tea, the baby is born without pain, *oui?*" *Oui, merci*, who would dare argue?

They slip out of the deep forest, timid and silent, barefoot or in flip-flops. They are poor, these midwives. Many do not even have teeth. Others eat nothing but tapioca flour. Helping humankind come into the world has never earned them a penny. "What I want most in this life of mine is a pretty bed," sighs sixty-six-year-old Cecília Forte, whose body has never known any resting place other than a cotton hammock. When hunger squeezes her gut, her heart gives way, threatening to stop. Made from tough hide, Cecília resists. She confesses she doesn't enjoy birthing all that much. "What I like most is mending old clothes. Why? Well, I think all old people like to mend clothes. It's a bit like mending life. Mending one to mend the other."

Delfina dos Santos, fifty-six, raises her hand to follow the path of babies she has caught. It is a dark, gnarly hand, both palms a tangle of lines weaving together all the lives she has welcomed. "I did Eremita's labors twice, Elvira's once, Odete once, Alzemira once, Leliane once, Helena twice, Celina once, Josefina once . . ." The trail of births goes on and on.

When she was fifteen, Maria Labonté helped her own mother give birth. Maria Rosalina dos Santos did her daughter's birth. Just like Nazira Narciso, forty-five, who likewise greeted her own granddaughter when the midwife refused to, because the girl's belly was "private." "She didn't have a husband," Nazira translates. How the baby was conceived, by dolphin or Holy Spirit, doesn't matter a bit: "God was the midwife." But he worked through a woman's hands, because childbirth, Nazira believes, "has to be done by an equal." "Indian, *crioula*, Brazilian, it's one pain," she explains. "The crying's the same."

Their hands of life grasp each other, their feet of many pathways unite in a circle inside the belly of the forest. The midwives thank the divinity at daybreak. Like all creatures in the world, the day emerges at a precise time, without anything or anyone needing to wrest it from night's womb. Day and child obey the same law, both contain the same seed, complementary parts of a single universe.

The midwives raise their candles, asking that light shine on their work. They invoke the earth, the river, the forest. This is talk among sisters, words hushed into the ear. The image speaks to a deaf society, oblivious to the umbilical cord, with something bigger than the world forged inside this world. The voice of Dorica, the oldest midwife in the forest, echoes through every woman when she declares: "It is time that makes man, and not man that makes time. Childbirth is mystery. And babies—we never pull them out. We just receive them."

The circle breaks up and the midwives climb into the boat to sail the rivers of Brazil's borderlands. They go to answer a call only they can hear.

BURIAL OF THE POOR

There is nothing sadder than the burial of the poor. Because the poor begin to be buried in life. So said Antonio, a man sculpted from the clay of a humility older than he. A man who is ashamed even to speak, and when he does, is afraid of speaking too loud. And when he lifts his eyes, he's worried that the mere boldness of lifting them will offend his boss right in the face. So said Antonio Antunes, who had just buried the casket of a son whose face he didn't know, a two-pound, one-ounce baby who died in his mother's belly. Antonio wanted a glimpse of his son's face, but the employee who went to fetch the child from the cooler wouldn't allow it. Antonio had purchased a little outfit for four dollars in downtown Porto Alegre so his son wouldn't be buried naked, like some animal's pup. But Antonio couldn't dress him. He was left with the small white casket that he cradled in his arms to grave number 2026 of Mercy Hospital's Holy Ground Cemetery.

When the dirt had covered his son's shallow grave, the father knew his own heart would remain unburied. Because at that instant Antonio Antunes realized that a shallow grave and a donated coffin, sown in a hillside cemetery, would be the fate shared by him, his children who survived him, and his grandchildren yet to come. Just as it had been the lot of his parents and grandparents before him. When he reached the foot of the hill at Holy Ground, after burying his nameless child, Antonio pronounced his sentence, head lowered, the flame in his eyes smothered by tears, by a rosary of pain that might well predate the discovery of Brazil. Antonio Antunes said:

"This is the path of the poor."

He said it with such anguish, with so much despair, that the words slashed through the burial grounds of poverty. Because a sentence only exists when it is an extension in letters of the soul of whoever utters it. It is the sum of words, and the tragedy held within them. Otherwise, it is just a sham of vowels and consonants, a waste of sound and space. And Antonio pronounced this phrase with such pain that even the thrush warbling on the other side of the wall fell silent, as if divining that this phrase of death was a man's life.

This report could end here, because everything has already been said. But sometimes a story has to be told more than one way if it is to be thoroughly understood.

There is nothing sadder than the burial of the poor because there is nothing worse than living and dying off others. There is nothing more brutal than having nothing of yours, not even a space for death. After a life without a place, having no place to die. After a life owning nothing, not owning even six feet under. For the poor, the ultimate tragedy is that even in death they don't escape life.

This is what Antonio Antunes, feller of trees, had come to understand. And this is what had finally broken him. Because this was just the beginning and because there was no end, only more of the same. Because men like Antonio are born and die the same way. In this sense, the baby who hadn't lived had merely saved time, relinquishing the interludes between all the forms of death reserved for him in life.

To understand the end, you have to understand the beginning. Antonio left the cemetery without any money for the bus fare back. Just like the fare out. He was guided by his sister-in-law, who put him up in Porto Alegre because he had traveled to the city from a coal-mining town. He'd been peeling bark off a eucalyptus tree on a Friday when his wife felt the warmth of blood running down her legs. She was keeping vigil over the health of her six-year-old daughter, a little girl who had never walked, and she told the young woman at the hospital what was happening in her belly. She was sent home with the explanation that it was nothing.

Saturday had barely dawned when Antonio carried his wife back to the clinic. Late that morning, after little had been done, Antonio overcame his atavistic meekness and threatened to call the cops. So the couple was dispatched to Porto Alegre, where they arrived too late. The mother was saved but the baby was dead. For how long, nobody knows. On Sunday their five-year-old son, who, like his sister, had never walked, went from an ambulance to the ICU at a hospital in the capital city. They learned he was suffering from pneumonia, although he'd been under treatment for something else for days. There he remained, his father dueling with death in the waiting room.

Monday had hardly dawned when Antonio went off to see to the burial of one child, throwing death off the scent of the other. He spent Monday between the hospital and the notary public office, back and forth more than once, because the hospital had forgotten to stamp the death certificate and have the doctor sign it. All of this, miles on foot because there was no money for the bus. All of this, on an empty stomach because there was no money for lunch. And all of this, with his sister-in-law, who had lost her own baby, stillborn, fifteen days earlier. With his sister-in-law who had buried her own son at Holy Ground fifteen days earlier. And from Monday to Tuesday, just one meal, rice and cabbage.

Nothing came to a close for Antonio Antunes when he reached the foot of the cemetery hill and uttered the phrase of his life. He had just buried a child who most likely would not have died if his father had not been poor. In a donated coffin, in a borrowed grave, on the hillside grounds of the only cemetery in the entire state capital that takes in the poor, and that for this reason alone deserves the eternal gratitude of all the Antonios.

Nothing came to a close for Antonio because he knows he'll be back shortly. And everything will remain as it is. As it always has been, in death as in life. He leaves behind his nameless child, buried in a shallow grave, no priest, no flowers. For the grave of the poor is less than six feet under, so it is easier to dispose of the body when the three-year limit is up. Then room must be made for another tiny child of the poor for another three years. And so it has gone for five hundred years.

Beneath each one of the more than two thousand crosses sown in the soft soil of Holy Ground Cemetery lies a fate like Antonio's. To comprehend the rest of the story, we must understand the death of the poor. We must understand that the biggest difference between a poor man's death and a rich man's is not the loneliness at one burial and the crowds at the other, the flowers missing at one and the pomp at the other, the plain wooden coffin at one and the cedar casket at the other. It's not even the swiftness of one and the slowness of the other.

The biggest difference is that the sadness at the burial of the poor lies less in their death and more in their life.

CRAZY

They say he's crazy. Ever since the first time he showed up at the gates of the beef, dairy, and horse expo early one morning, they've said he's crazy. He arrived bone-weary and hungry. Very hungry. It was 1991 and he was fifteen. He had come from the city of Uruguaiana, on Brazil's border with Argentina. Some he traveled by foot, some squeezed between animals on the hindquarters of a truck. It took him three days to get there, but he made it.

He showed up early one morning at the expo gates with a broomstick and introduced it as his horse. He asked for a health certificate so the animal could set hoof in the show. He put his hobbyhorse through the paces and performed all the movements required in the Golden Bridle competition, the grand prize for the Crioulo breed. Thus he inaugurated his participation at Expointer, the great festival of Rio Grande do Sul, the Brazilian state so far south that it almost slides down into Uruguay. There, the locals are called *gaúchos*, a centuries-old name given to men who rode bareback, roaming the pampas, losing themselves to find themselves in the "horizontal vertigo" of the plains.

His name is Vanderlei Ferreira. He was born into a poor family and never went to school, but now he attends the School of Animal Science. Every year they shave his head as if he were a freshman. He sits in on classes, sometimes even takes tests. If his outlook on life were less figurative, he would discover he's illiterate. But since he has decided his metric is a broomstick, he's going to get his college diploma.

Vanderlei lives in Uruguaiana, where he's part of the local folklore. He sleeps in hiding at a gas station or sometimes at an uncle's house. He once made a VW van his residence. Whatever his roost, he has chosen to remain forever in the borderlands, but without borders, gazing at vast herds of cattle through his ranch-house window. He manages to see, feel, and touch all of this while wrapped in an old blanket in the corner of nowhere. When he wakes up, he grabs a toy cell phone, plants himself at the door of the Banco do Brasil, and orders the foreman: "Load the cattle."

Ever since he discovered Rio Grande do Sul's largest expo, he hasn't missed a single one. He arrives stinking of animals, fleas grazing on his scalp. The veterinarians give him a shower, disinfect his leather, and even present him with a pair of boots. Other benefactors scattered about the expo share a bit of barbecue and provide him with a hat and a pair of *bombachas*, the baggy trousers worn in the pampas. Dressed in a white vet's smock, he goes around with a clipboard under his arm. At night he sleeps in a stall in the quarantine barn, between sick mares and bulls, while he spends the day galloping through the expo grounds. Or he leaves his horse neighing at the door of some exhibitor and goes off to recite in some girl's ear: "Ducks lose their feathers, fish lose their scales, and I waste time loving someone who doesn't love me."

When his wooden horse starts bucking, people laugh and get a kick out of it. The madman laughs too, and hard.

Etymologist Joan Corominas defined the *gaúcho* as of uncertain origin, a motherless calf, orphaned, poor and indigent. A vagabond, according to the scholar José de Saldanha. A man who doesn't know how to go by foot, says Félix de Azara. In the words of Carlos Reverbel, he's a "trail-hand on the paths of adventure, wrangler of dreams and dangers . . . master of himself, rover of broad horizons, companion of freedom."

If all of this is the *gaúcho*, there is no one at the expo more authentic than the madman. It's possible that he takes the myth more seriously than anyone else. It's possible that the only thing left for *gaúchos* like him is a hobbyhorse. It's possible that all that's left of utopia is a broomstick. It's even possible he's so crazy that he invented a *gaúcho*.

I pull my horse alongside his. "Vanderlei, are you crazy?"

He looks at me as if I were the crazy one. He hits his fist against his head, urging me to use my brain. I try.

"Why did you come to Expointer?"

"At college, in Uruguaiana, I heard us students were excused to go. It was 1991. I charged off on foot."

"But that's more than 350 miles. Was it hard?"

"It was the worst thing in my life. Nobody wanted to bring me. I went hungry. It took me three days to get here. But one morning here I was."

"And what did you think?"

"It was the best day of my life. I was terrified by a whole bunch of things. I wanted it to never end."

"And your horse?"

"My horse is a broom. I wish it was a real champion, like BT Faceiro do Junco, but it's a broomstick."

"If you know it's a broomstick, what are you thinking when you're mounted on it?"

"I dream I'm on a real horse. Carrying a pretty girl on its haunches. Lassoing, digging in my spurs . . ."

"What's your horse like?"

"He's dappled. White."

"And what do you do with your horse?"

"I parade with him, ride the tests. One time, in Uruguaiana, they scored me on everything. I did everything you do for the Golden Bridle. I've paraded down the avenue too. They gave me a standing ovation."

"What would your girl be like?"

"I'd like a girl who's not demanding. One who, when I wanted to go out, would say I was free to go."

"Sometimes you sleep in a car outside a gas station. What do you think about?"

"I think I'm on a ranch with my girl."

"Have you ever worked as a cowhand?"

"I started to, but they wanted me to get up at four a.m. to do stuff I could do at six. It didn't work out."

"So a cowhand's life isn't any good?"

"It's real tough. A guy suffers, gets hurt, and on top of it doesn't make much. I don't want to be a cowhand. I want to be a veterinarian."

"Are you going to college?"

"I attend classes, learn a bit of everything. But I don't know how to read or write. Just numbers."

"When did you get to Expointer, this last time?"

"I got here Friday. Came by truck, with some purebred bulls. There was a little room left."

"And when the expo is over?"

"It leaves my heart sad."

"What's the sadness like?"

"It's a deep sadness."

"How do you leave?"

"I leave sad, lying down, pensive. I go back with the animals."

"Do you only ride horseback at the expo?"

"I've never walked."

"Have you ever mounted a real horse?"

"Once."

"And what did you think?"

"It's much better than a broomstick."

"You know this is a fantasy, that the horse is a broomstick. And even so you gallop around on a broomstick. Why?"

"Unless you make things up, life's no fun. It all gets real tough."

"Some people think you're crazy."

"Truth is, people who think I'm crazy aren't reasoning things out."

It took me a few years to realize that the *gaúcho* on the hobbyhorse had provided me with the finest definition of human life: We all have a broomstick and wish we had a horse. Life is this movement, always incomplete, between the broomstick and the horse.

THE NOISE

We'll call him T. here.

The first time I saw him, it was his eyes that captured me. They were the eyes of a man who has discovered something he finds extremely hard to believe, the look of someone who can finally see, but hasn't processed things yet. A look forever surprised and at the same time skeptical, hoping that anytime now someone will assure him it has all been a mistake, restore his faith, and his world will go back to spinning the right way around. "They knew, the whole time they knew they were killing us. And they kept on killing us," he said. He didn't look at me, but at a place between inside and out, where he seemed to be trapped.

I was at his home in Greater São Paulo, and after this sentence he fell quiet. His silence was sweltering though it wasn't a hot day; it was only his silence generating heat. At first I heard it very soft. The noise had been there but, like the buzzing of a mosquito you don't notice right away, I had been deaf to it. I sought out the cause, far from his ravaged eyes. The noise grew louder, and suddenly I had no idea how I hadn't heard it before. My ears took me to his chest, covered by a shirt so well ironed that it still bore pleats.

For a moment, I absorbed myself in the shirt, which had moved me. I had seen such shirts on other bodies before. They were the shirts of poor men, of poor workers, and every one of those shirts had held an immense exertion, the size of an entire life. The cut was bad but the fabric was of good quality, outmoded print aside. The shirt had something of an urge for church about it. It had seen much wear but was clean and had been meticulously ironed by a wife who loved her husband, so that her man would look good for the reporter, so he'd look respectable. And, more than anything else, so he would look like what he was, a gainfully employed worker, his whole life at the same company.

The shirt also conveyed a poor man's dread, of being labeled shiftless. Constantly humiliated by the police, always having to prove he isn't a thief, hasn't killed anyone, doesn't sleep during the day, doesn't malinger, isn't the wrong person at the wrong time, struggling to prove his innocence day after day, order above the order. A similar story was told by his wedding shoes, black, with pointy toes, awkward on feet accustomed to thick-soled shoes meant for a factory floor. But they fit the occasion, his wife would have assured him. A reporter is almost an authority, much like a VIP, and as soon as he'd opened the door, before his eyes returned to the place that they only left if he was startled, to quickly return again, he had held his employment book out to me. Mine has rarely left the drawer; it has never been a source of any pride. But his, the poor worker's employment book, was evidence, the shield that defended him in a society where he had been born under the sign of suspicion.

We were still standing. And I, always embarrassed by that gesture, blocked the little blue book with a gentle movement of my hand. You don't need to show me, I said. I believe you, sir. And he, visibly frustrated, made me sit down on a love seat, while he pulled up a chair with a cane seat for himself. I asked to switch places, explaining that I would rather sit up straighter to write. He didn't understand, but agreed. Then he put his blue book on the end table between us, next to a vase of plastic roses, an image of Our Lady of Aparecida, and a frame where a smiling family posed in front of one of those wedding cakes decorated with huge pink icing flowers (daisies perhaps?) and two little figurines, bride and groom. He laid the book down carefully, as if it might suffer an injury at his hands, coarsened by machines. And there it stayed, like a monument protecting him from me as well.

But I've gotten distracted. I was trying to find the noise that had taken me to the small white buttons on his shirt. Underneath them, his chest moved in painful slowness. Now the sound was almost a roar. Why hadn't I noticed it before? From that moment on, I always found myself confronting it, hearing his chest rise and fall, as if his lungs wanted to envelop every bit of air with each intake of breath but failed each time. Like a fish out of water, I thought, trying unsuccessfully to breathe. A fish that will die the next minute, and knows it. His steady stare had the same look a fish has when it is tossed on a riverbank, cast abruptly from the world it knows.

Suddenly, the noise I had taken so long to hear overpowered the room, and it seemed it would drown out his voice when he resumed talking. The sound was soon unbearable and for just a moment I searched for a button where I could turn it off, as if it were a ceiling fan in an old courtroom drama. I knew I'd never be free from this sound, just as I would never be free from that look. And now, having emerged from his daze, he was staring at me. "Can you hear it?" How could he know? I was embarrassed. "I heard it for the first time one night when I couldn't dance with my wife. We were at a dance, and everybody knew I was good on my feet. I was getting ready to put on a show, but after a few spins I had to stop. I ran out of breath."

I listened to him, and I also listened to the broken sound of his chest. I wanted to flee, but forced myself to remain seated. He didn't seem to notice my uneasiness. T. wanted to talk, and I should want to listen. But I just wanted to escape the noise, which was starting to suffocate me as well. "It was a bolero. 'Solamente una vez,' you know it?" And he sang it softly, oblivious to me. "*Solamente una vez amé en la vida. Solamente una vez y nada más . . .*" Exhausted, he paused before returning to the dance hall. "Sitting there at the table, I didn't hear the lyrics anymore. I only heard the thing inside me, the thing that steals my air." Thing? I repeated, questioning gently, like a psychoanalyst punctuating his discourse in the sterile environment of a doctor's office.

"The thing, you know, the asbestos," and he looked at me again. He rubbed his chest gently with his big hand, his middle finger twisted from some injury. A labor accident perhaps. I made a note on my pad to ask later. "It's inside me. I'm going to die and it'll stay inside me." He seemed to get lost again.

His wife came in with coffee on a tray, a plate garnished with cookies. "To make life a little sweeter," she said. I smiled, grateful. Only then did I feel like crying. Not because of the horror-struck man before me, but because of the cups adorned with tiny flowers that reminded me of my grandmother's kitchen. Because of the cookies, which, when I was a child, were also "for visitors." Because of her hair, which I imagined she had fixed up to make a good impression on me. Then she gave herself permission to sit down beside him on the sofa. Almost on the edge, unsure if she should be there but risking it.

T. didn't seem to notice her at his side. He kept on talking, as if he were speaking not to me but to someone who existed only inside him. "When the plant opened up here, everybody wanted a job. It was big and people thought it was nice. It was progress arriving. And we wanted to be part of it. I was young, my family had come from the countryside for a better life in the city, and I thought I could advance with the company if I did everything right. You know, grow with the company. That's what we thought back then. And I think I did advance." He took in his house with a sweeping motion that required both hands. The simple but well-built brick house grew bigger when I saw it through his eyes. Hesitating over her first sentence, his wife completed the thought. "We wanted to get married, you know, but my father would only agree if he had a good job. So the factory was all our hope."

Now she was confident, her back sunk into the velvet-like floral upholstery but her body pushed forward, her hands fidgeting above the tiny blue flowers on her dress. This is a woman who loves flowers, I thought. But there were no fresh ones in the house. "Her father wanted someone with a better position in life. He was a strict man, the old-fashioned kind. He wanted her to marry a guy in the military." He took a short break in pursuit of air. "But she'd danced with me one night, and she could never look at anyone else again."

Now he laughed, seductive, his eyes softening, and I caught sight of the man he had been. "You know, he really was a good dancer," she went on, animated. "All my girlfriends wanted to dance with him." She blushed a little, her cheeks still virginal after all these years. "I wanted to marry someone in the military too, because of the swords, you know. That's not from your time, you're still real young." She smiled, glancing to see if the compliment had pleased me. I made a gesture that said "I'm not all that young," accompanied by a half smile. Satisfied, she went on. "When a military man got married, the others would line up and raise their swords, and the newlyweds would walk under them. It was the prettiest wedding, you know, we all wanted one." What happened? I asked. "I think I fell in love because he was the best *bailador*." And she shook with a sheepish laugh.

I had never heard that word before, *bailador*—dancer—and I

underlined it on my pad to remind myself of it when I went to write the story. But she was already moving on. She talked much faster than he did, swallowing some syllables in her eagerness to avoid interruption. "The others envied me because I danced with him all night long. He was rather handsome, he had these eyes, you know, but without the wrinkles. And he was quite the smooth talker, oh, he was." I stopped listening to her for an instant, trying to make out what she had seen in his eyes in the past. But I couldn't get beyond the darkness of his gaze in the present. I dropped my pen on the floor, so like me when I get rattled. She didn't notice, but kept on talking. "I was silly back then, but I was lucky. He was a hard worker and we were happy, you know." She was the type who used "you know" as a linguistic crutch to back up her efforts. And she made a big effort. "At least until we found out." She lowered her voice and her eyes, and the time for smiles was over.

I waited, his chest rising and falling like an old car on a steep hill. And the noise. I tried to imagine how the woman could stand spending the night listening to that sound in the chest of the man she loved, wanting to turn it off but knowing the sound would stop only when he died; knowing that the noise was the best sound she would hear forever, and forever was growing shorter every day. I looked at her in alarm, and I thought she had heard inside my head, because she sank back into the sofa, as if wanting to burrow into it.

The atmosphere overwhelmed me, crushing me in a stifling paralysis. Going against my firm belief that silence must be tolerated in order to hear the Other, I asked a reckless question, in a voice louder than I would have liked. Now I sounded so much like a reporter. Direct, objective. When did you find out the asbestos was killing you? He was startled, as if it took a bit to register the change in pace. "When?" Who, what, where, when, why, and how—the six questions a journalism student learns at school, to be answered right at the beginning of a story. As if it were possible to answer them in a handful of sentences, as if they told something essential. What was essential was the noise, and it did not become words.

"The first guys started getting sick, but we didn't know one thing had anything to do with another. It's not like that virus, Ebola. It's slow, you start losing your wind, start getting tired, until you can't even go to the bakery for bread anymore. Or dance." T. spoke like an automaton, and I knew he was making an effort to answer, but he wasn't there. "You've got to understand." And now he looked at me again, but still didn't seem to see me. "The factory was our mother, that's how we saw it. It was like a big family. That's what they told us, and we thought that's how it really was. A job at the factory was admired in the city. We were proud. I carried the factory in my bosom, you know?" He paused to recover his breath. Did he realize he did indeed carry the factory in his bosom now? He did, I soon learned. "We were really proud, and I can't lie, I liked working there. My whole life was there, I raised my kids there, I felt a sense of satisfaction when I took my boys to the factory and said I worked there. It was a man's job. How was I supposed to know I carried the factory in my bosom, but in another way?" He returned to his look of limbo.

I had it wrong. T. was not completely there, but there and here. He was still telling a story, even though he knew the story could never be told in its entirety. It was a bit like breathing. The air got harder and harder to reach, but he still managed to capture enough to stay alive. When he quit talking, it wasn't just because he was returning to his horror, but because he ran out of breath. T. was exhausted. The twentieth century had betrayed him.

The prostrated worker before me was a worker from a failed modernity. Illusions of progress and power had vanished with the air. His body had reached the twenty-first century like a corroded planet. But he was the first to pay the price, starting with the discovery that he had built a life out of smoke. Smoke, no—powder.

Asbestos powder. And now the truth condemned him. It wasn't just his concrete existence that he was losing, but everything he believed he was and had lived. The factory was one of dozens that asbestos multinationals had scattered around the world, including in Brazil. The family-factory, which took care of him and theirs, was a symbolic construct. The factory, the very real, monstrous machinery, did not see him as a son. If there was a mother, she was a Medea. The plant owners, those gentlemen so far away, their names foreign, only saw bones and muscles in him and men like him. It was literally with his flesh that they had fed one of the most successful twentieth-century industries. The day they opened the plant in town, the mighty asbestos emperors knew full well that when those men stepped through the factory gates, little blue books clutched proudly in their hands, they were almost certainly condemned to suffocate to death. Or to die of the aggressive, always fatal asbestos cancer, mesothelioma. Going into the factory was taking the first step down death row. And the plant owners knew it.

"It took me a long time to believe they knew. It took all of us time. Even sick, even winded, we still took a long time to believe it," he said, speaking again, and his voice was so low I had to lean forward to hear him. When did you believe it? I asked softly. Instead of answering, he put three spoons of sugar in a cup, in no hurry, as if searching for the answer inside some internal file. He poured coffee and then stirred it with a little spoon. He lifted the cup to his lips, his hand shaking, and took a very slow sip, as if it were the most important thing in the world. Only then did I notice the colored stone at the tip of the spoon handle, again like the ones from my childhood. And for a moment I escaped by turning the stone into a madeleine.

Then his voice ripped into my daydream like a knife, bringing me back. "I was only certain when they knocked here at this door," he pointed toward the entrance to his house, "offering me money to sign a piece of paper where I'd give up the right to sue the company." Did you sign it? I interrupted, my anxiety misplaced. He looked at me and for the first time I saw the hate there. It was so dark that I squirmed, as if I couldn't get comfortable in the chair. Later they would tell me his eyes were blue, and I wouldn't believe them. They were, they assured me, but that's not what I saw. There was no heaven in those eyes, only hell.

His wife put her hand on his knee, as if to soothe him. Once again he didn't seem to notice. Yet he tore the pen from my hand in one quick move and gripping it said, "No. I'm never going to sign. And I'm never going to settle either. They'll have to admit that they killed us. The court is going to force them to admit what they did to us. I'm going to die, but the whole world is going to know they're murderers."

Without waiting a second for him to catch his breath, I thrust in. And if there's no justice? I knew I was being cruel, that his outburst had been a supreme show of strength, his ultimate attempt to die like a man. But I had to ask the question, because I knew there wouldn't be any justice. Not in his lifetime at least, and maybe never. I recalled the ruling a judge had handed down to a worker who had sought compensation after losing a lung to an asbestos disease. The judge had declared: it's possible to live with only one lung. I would later realize I should have kept quiet. That he too knew he would be defeated, but that justice was all the hope he could have, and that I had no right to do anything to shake such a fragile illusion. But I hadn't grown old enough yet to know how to touch the delicacy of a human life so close to death. Even so, he didn't seem to hear me. His chest roared with the sound and the fury of a Shakespearean play.

He stood up. One of the cups fell to the floor as if in slow motion. It shattered, and still he didn't hear it. "Everything here is asbestos. My house is asbestos. They gave me asbestos to mix in with the cement, to make the walls and the slabs in our yard. There's asbestos in my roof, my water reservoir is made of asbestos. They gave it to me and I thanked them! And, you want to know something, I'm not ashamed to say it, even my underwear was made from asbestos bags, dyed blue."

He grimaced as he talked, and for the first time I noticed his cheeks were sunken and all of him was covered in grayish white, a skeleton-man covered with a fine, almost transparent skin. "I took my kids to play in the gray dust. They thought it was pretty. It was a happy day, we didn't know. And maybe I condemned my kids to die. Me. My own kids. But I didn't know." For the first time his dark eyes floated in salt water. But he didn't stop. His speech was now a river, a current. "My wife spent her whole life washing my asbestos-drenched clothes in the basin. My wife might be next. I'm a condemned man because I condemned my family, do you understand that?" I understood yet couldn't fathom it, and never would. "It might be even worse for them, it might be asbestos cancer, what's it called?" Mesothelioma, I said in a whisper, as if the horrendous disease might take shape and materialize among us.

I remembered Romana Blasotti Pavesi, the old woman from Casale Monferrato, the Italian city contaminated by asbestos, who lost her husband and daughter to mesothelioma, the child they had one day taken to see the pretty whirling dust. Romana, who also lost her sister, a cousin, and a nephew to mesothelioma. Romana, who lived alone in an apartment inhabited only by knickknacks and souvenirs, and who sometimes pulled a box from her closet, retrieving from it a long multihued plait of red hair. Her daughter's. And she would caress it in her nameless pain.

T. had sat down again. I thought he would return to that place between outside and in, but he didn't. Once more he took the pen from my hand, gently this time, and I offered no resistance. He looked at it, and for a moment I thought he would break it. But T.

just handed it back to me, in an almost solemn gesture, as if he were only now granting me permission. He said: "Write this down."

I sat up straight, an instinctive movement. And he declared, pronouncing every syllable with his dark eyes fixed on me:

"I am made of asbestos."

He put his hand on his chest. His wife was crying softly now, while she picked up the broken bits of cup, the tiny flowers smashed. Not even dead flowers escaped death in this house. I nodded, mute. The thing, the thing inside him. I was familiar with asbestosis, I had studied it. The fiber was inhaled and it settled in the lungs, where it couldn't be ripped out. Settled in, no—it staked itself there, producing a lesion. The body reacted in order to heal itself. But the fiber went on with its wounding, and the body kept on trying to heal. Over time, over years, the lung turned into a scar and could no longer fulfill its purpose, no longer able to inhale and exhale. Slowly, progressively, that is what was happening inside the man in front of me, a process that could not be held back. T. was nearing the moment when his lung itself would be suffocated, shackled by scar tissue. "Stone lung" was what they called it. Then T. would die in terror, his brain ordering air to be sucked in, his lung unable to move. And it would all be over.

I should have kept quiet, excused myself, and left. But I didn't know how to leave, and I've never again known. Somehow I, too, was trapped, and desperate to cover up the sound of that moribund lung. Then I did the unforgiveable. I repeated the question that never should have been asked. I got it wrong twice. "And what if there is no justice?" He cast a long vacant look at me, as if he hadn't understood the question. His wife interrupted, trying to save us. "Would you like some fresh coffee?" She attempted a smile. I almost hugged her. "I can make it in an instant." She got up, carrying the garden on her dress, leaving us alone and withered.

He set his eyes on me again, and now his look was simply sad.

His sorrow hurt me more than his hatred. I opened my mouth to ask any other question, even if to comment on the weather, ask if it was going to rain, but he motioned for me to be quiet, and he said, "If there's no justice, I won't die like a man."

"You'll die like what, then?" I asked.

"I'll die like an ant."

I didn't ask why an ant. He was beyond words. Dozens of miles later, back at my home, I continued to hear the noise. All of the letters I have set down here have failed. They reveal nothing other than how impossible it is to express the sound of his breathing.

Horror refuses to be spoken.

Three years later.

T. had been tied to an oxygen tank for a hundred days. A representative from the asbestos multinational came to the hospital with a document for him to sign. If he didn't sign, his family wouldn't get one penny in damages. If they signed, they would get just short of $11,000. "It's almost three times what we offered you before," the man said. "You'll get more than your colleagues." T. was in his final throes. I wonder if that fellow standing there in front of him, dressed in a suit and tie, holding out a pen and piece of paper, heard the man's chest. T. signed.

The noise stopped the night the check cleared.

A COUNTRY CALLED BRASILÂNDIA

If the ashes in her pipe turn black, it's a no-go. If they turn white, then this report will come off. Dona Eugênia, seventy-six, puffs her way around me. This test, she tells me, is 100 percent on the mark. Her spirit guide Preto Velho whispers things in her ear, she says, things that happen. She's had this gravelly male voice tucked in her throat since she was a girl. Faith healer and cartomancer, Dona Eugênia wields the piercing eyes of an X-ray. Now she looks at the ashes. And at me. And at the ashes. "They've gone white," she says. "Good energy." Only then does Dona Eugênia open the doors of Brasilândia, her heart, and her home.

The idea is for me to spend some days living on the north side of São Paulo in this enclave of 250,000 inhabitants, recently upgraded to a movie set. The community used to be considered ugly, dirty, mean. But since serving as the location for both a film and a television series, it has become trendy. Or, to quote Tata Amaral, director of *Antônia*, the latest feature-length movie shot here, "photogenic." Brasilândia embodies the Brazilian periphery, as singer Sandra Sá puts it succinctly.

This dispatch reveals what has always been here, concealed by violence. For this is another of the favela's tragedies: corpses lie out in the open, while what lies hidden is delicacy. Day after day, like the kites that boys doggedly struggle to free from jumbled wires and fly up to the sky, tenderness is wrested from concrete so that life becomes possible. Or else no one could take it. A kite tangled up in wires is an apprenticeship for a poor boy headed into the future.

Antônia is the tale of four girls from a rap group on the outskirts of São Paulo who share the dream of scaling one stage after the other. It is a movie about friendship, the sentiment that lets you dream even in geographies supposedly bereft of hope. This point of view unveils what the city next door, split off from the favela by alarm and fear, fails to see. Beyond the violence, the power of human passions crushes, indeed liquefies, the hardness of an everyday life in concrete. And here, concrete is a concept as much as it is the building material used for this gray, almost treeless architecture.

Cultural forays into the periphery have become unrelenting. Some favelas have turned into sightseeing stops, but as attractions on display, falsely tamed for tourists, they are misleading. What happens on the urban periphery is still so removed from the Brazil of the core that it seems like another geography, and the middle class continues to fear the people who live here as if they were a horde of barbarians ready to charge down the hill. In this sense, Brasilândia is as far from São Paulo as the Amazon.

Living in Brasilândia as a foreigner, I'm driven to vertigo by this optical illusion. My own home is so close, just over there. Yet only a few hours into this experience, I feel split off, like everyone else. It is truly a feeling of exile, expressed in how people here speak of a city that is inaccessible, although officially theirs as well, on maps at least. "Paulista Avenue is the city of luxury. Brasilândia is the city of the Brazilian people. On Paulista, nobody gives anybody anything. Here we share. There, nobody sees me. Here, everyone says hi to me," says Ailton Barroso, referring to the pulsing heart of São Paulo, Avenida Paulista. Ailton owns a concrete slab rooftop that affords one of the best views of the capital. On New Year's Eve, he lends out his skybox for the fireworks display over Paulista. His eyes touch the outlines of the buildings along the avenue, but Ailton carries a divided city within him.

Brasilândia was born as a land of expatriation. More than sixty years ago, something happened where Avenida Ipiranga crosses Avenida São João: residents there were driven out of downtown for the widening of the iconic intersection from Caetano Veloso's song "Sampa." They carved Brasilândia out of old farms and much virgin forest. One of these properties belonged to Brasílio Simões. It is because of this *cachaça* maker, and not Brazil, that the community bears a name that enables it to shelter an entire country.

Privacy? Fat Chance!

Dona Eugênia has reserved the only bedroom in her house for me. She swears she sleeps on the living room couch because she likes to watch back-to-back programs on her eight-inch TV into the early hours. From the bookcase, a porcelain ballerina, Puff the Bear, and more than a dozen knickknacks that were rounded up at bingo watch over her slumber. We sleep with the door unlatched. It is ironic that in a city like São Paulo, so filled with fear, it is in a favela that you can spend the night with your doors unlocked and wake up alive the next day.

I have a double bed, five pillows, and a pink satin bedspread all to myself. Dona Eugênia is pampering me. But mainly she's making a concession to the privacy so dear to the class I come from—a concept that makes no sense in Brasa, as the community is known among those close to it.

Favelas are a collective manifestation. Daily life takes place entirely in the streets, in public space, and this public space includes the inside of homes. Doors are always open and it is not rude to enter without knocking. Each person's life only makes sense if it is shared with the neighbors. In a city where people are leery of getting involved with strangers (and even with acquaintances), the favela is a paradigm of solidarity.

Dona Eugênia says over and over that there is no shortage of food in her house, and at breakfast she piles my plate high with slices of ham and cheese. It is vital for her to show me that although she's poor, there is plenty on her table. There's no concern about cholesterol or triglycerides, none of this salad and lean meat stuff. It's a feast of black beans, rice, sausage, and lots of sauce. Dona Eugênia only gets grumpy when she discovers I've brought along some soap. Do I think there's no hand soap at her place? Dona Eugênia had set aside a special bar for me, nice and fragrant.

Tuca, Dona Eugênia's daughter, descends from the upper premises, cigarette already dangling from her lips. Brasilândia has practically no houses or apartments. It has "familial architectural complexes," as Tata Amaral calls them. When a son decides to get married, he advances across the hill, upward and sideways. Every unit is connected to others by rickety stairs. Anyone who can rents out one of their rooms to make a little extra. That's Brasa's middle class.

Dona Eugênia used to rent a back room to a prostitute who was dating a guy from First Capital Command, the biggest criminal gang in Brazil. Her tenant crossed paths with the other São Paulo every night out of professional necessity and came back with intriguing tales. Late one night she scrambled up the slab rooftop euphoric because she and a coworker had fleeced one of the country's hottest soap opera stars. The young lady eventually moved to another complex at the request of Dona Eugênia, who thought she was too noisy. Her boyfriend was executed some months back. The latest addition to the family complex is now being remodeled to make room for Dona Eugênia's grandson, who is getting married.

The West's current gender crisis over the role played by men acquires its own tones on the periphery. Every morning the streets grow crowded with fathers beaten down by joblessness, drinking at bars or on street corners. But there are no unoccupied women. Most do not have formal jobs, but they turn themselves outside in, doing a thousand and one things to pay the bills and support children who are already into their twenties and have acquired more education but can't find jobs. Their frustrated mothers are left with the hope that closed doors will open "with a computer class." So they find yet another odd job to cover the monthly fees at one of the questionable-looking information technology courses that are popping up around the neighborhood, and make plans to purchase a desktop on credit.

Dona Eugênia's daughter Tuca is one of those women who does a bit of everything. She starts her day by placing a bet in Brazil's popular, and illegal, animal lottery. If she's dreamed about her brother-in-law, she bets on the pig and donkey. Evidently her relative brings good luck, as Tuca won the bookcase in her home with this tip. The numbers ticket itself is priceless, all politically correct: "Say 'no' to drugs." Tuca makes chocolate eggs at Easter, holiday baskets for Christmas and New Year's, and cakes for the wives, mothers, and daughters of inmates to sweeten visiting hours. She takes blood pressure, gives injections, and cares for the ill. She sells legitimate French perfume, passed along to her by friends who work at import agencies. You have to earn more than the minimum wage to shell out seventy to a hundred and fifty dollars on a bottle of Chanel or Dior, so Tuca's clientele belong to the local elites: a guy who clones bank cards and a big-time drug dealer. She saves a new Givenchy release for the latter.

Tuca exhausts herself to pay her bills on time and keep her name clean, but she doesn't handpick her clients. This is an explicit rule of coexistence in the favela: what you do to make your living is a personal matter. Everything else is up for public consumption. When Tuca's oldest son showed up at home with drugs, she called the boy's father and had him hand the goods back over to the dealer. It was time to draw a line in the sand. Business boundaries were set.

One Sunday, a patrol car made a blatant appearance down at the corner, right in the middle of the street. The cops paid no attention to the gambling payoffs taking place right in front of them. The only thing missing from the scene was for the bookie to get more comfortable by leaning against the bumper. Half an hour later, the cops squealed off. A phone rang immediately in a house nearby. On the other end of the line was a gentleman who is very well respected in Brasa, but who engages in activities subject to the penal code. "Could you see what precinct the car was from? Because if it was X, I already paid them."

Sundays drag by in Brasilândia like anywhere else in the world. The only thing to look forward to is the evening rehearsal of the Rosas de Ouro samba school. Brasa is into samba, *pagode*, and *forró* much more than rap. When a sneak preview of *Antônia* was screened in the community, nonstop drumming could be heard in the background, even when the girls were rapping. The audience members strained their brains trying to uncover clues to what Tata Amaral was trying to say; some left with theories, others with migraines. It turned out a Carnival group had been rehearsing right next door to the makeshift cinema, asserting the rhythm of Brasa's beating heart.

Bright and early Monday morning, Edimar, fifty-seven years old, thirteen children and sixteen grandchildren, lands at the counter of the corner bar, infused with the sound of Brazil, *balacobaco*, *ziriguidum*, *telecoteco*. "Here's where my genesis lies, miss: my blue-eyed Portuguese grandpa grabbed my big black grandma, and the result was this good-for-nothing here." First he explains his roots, then his goal: "I came here to buy some mints. Married almost forty years, and the old lady still complains about my kerosene breath."

Partying without Anorexia

As soon as twenty-one-year-old Adriana's belly started filling out because she had been dating twenty-four-year-old Luizinho, the neighborhood moved into action. The unemployed girl had been a virgin and her fiancé, a janitor, neither smoked nor drank. A lean purse wasn't going to deny them a wedding reception. The girl's mother had been quick to warn that cohabitation was out of the question. Luizinho would march into the justice of the peace's office with his best foot forward, even if he had to borrow shoes.

Knowing this, Tuca quickly sequestered her oldest son's dancing "leathers" and dispatched them to the bridegroom's house. She took charge of the black bean stew for lunch, the pulled beef, snacks, and wedding cake. Adriana's best friend bought the ingredients for the cake. A peddler uncle contributed coconut bars, peanuts, ground peanut candy, and ice cream. Another neighbor chipped in half a dozen bottles of soda. Adriana's sister-in-law took care of the wedding dress. A neighbor lent them his fancy car, a 1996 navy blue Ford Mondeo.

Adriana chose a couple who work as street vendors on São Paulo's east side for her witnesses. They were upset because their earnings had plummeted after e-tickets had replaced paper travel and meal vouchers, which kept them from giving the newlyweds a more fitting gift. Luizinho picked a relative involved in nondeclarable activities, plus his own mother. But when it came time to sign the marriage license, it was discovered that Dona Marlene didn't have any identification. There was a commotion. To prevent the wedding from imploding for lack of a documented witness, this reporter signed the certificate. All for the sake of a happy ending.

The door to the bride's grandmother's house was left open. Anyone could walk in. But the drunken fellow's legs wouldn't carry him across the street, so someone took him over a plate of food. In Brasa, there's no such thing as a gate-crasher. Or anorexia. Every plate was heaped high with rice, kale, and bean stew balanced as perilously as the additions to the houses. Then came seconds, and thirds . . . then the cake, and another cake . . . and bread with meat and more bread. There's always room for more bread, another slice of cake, another bit of pig's ear.

The party soon spilled into the street, where twelve-year-old Rafael was recounting his epic journey as a boy from the urban periphery. He had caught a ride on a delivery truck to discover the ocean, but he didn't get there until nighttime. Still, he got his feet wet. He was broadcasting his big news to the whole street: "The ocean is mega-ginormous!"

Luizinho, Adriana, her sister, and a niece went to share the clambering top floor of a family complex comprising seven houses that mount dangerously toward heaven. Luizinho plugged the leaks in the roof, laid down flooring, and painted the walls cream and white. Next he scattered Adriana's stuffed bears across the bed. The couple caught a bus and got off at the closest Casas Bahia department store. They found a bargain on clearance and arranged to buy their bedroom furniture over nine months. Then they secured their wedding rings at a watch store in the neighborhood of Lapa, with payment to be made in six installments. Their wedding night was spent playing twenty-five-cent bingo.

Real Hot Dogs

There is a lot of loving in Brasilândia, with the intensity of those who put love above all other aspirations. There are no middle-class dilemmas of the what-about-my-career type. Love is unbridled. This holds for people, this holds for dogs.

Piti is a pinscher, the tiny kind, wide-eyed, pointed ears, yappy bark. We look at each other skeptically. It is my intent to ignore him the rest of my days in Brasa. But I'm a newcomer and haven't yet grasped something vital. Here, dogs are human. At the age of four, hardly young for a dog, Piti really wants to lose his virginity but hasn't managed it. I warn him to keep away from my pillow. Piti growls. He becomes a *Canis erectus*.

His plight has touched Brasilândia. They tried a female poodle; she rejected him. They brought in a Chihuahua; she couldn't take the weight. Now they're trying a mongrel, but for some unfathomable reason, Piti fails. He hides leftover food under living room cushions and eats communion wafers brought from church. Freud would say that Piti has developed hysteria. The truth is, Piti is suffering. Worse yet, he suffers in the public eye. Every living soul who passes by the gate calls up to Tuca, Piti's owner: "Nothing yet?" And walks away shaking his or her head.

On the eve of her daughter's wedding, Célia cries. Her husband lost his job and has turned into a drunk, "practically a beggar." She is a manicurist who also sells lingerie, beauty creams, and natural medicine. "I'm a hustler," she explains. She just can't kick her husband out, because she loves him. "My mom used to rent out a room, right here in this house. I opened the door and fell under his spell. I felt something, and he did too. We stood there staring at each other. Both of us had set wedding dates with other people, but he covered up his commitment ring, and I just trembled." Célia says it, and trembles. And then cries. When her husband comes in, a tottering shell of what he once was, he can still recall the color of the dress she was wearing the first time he saw her: "Red, with little straps."

Elza the seamstress fled finer pastures for love and landed in Brasilândia. Her dog, Fany, has a long red coat. She has fallen in love with the mutt Requenguela, a freeloading fellow who is not worth what he eats—in his case, two hot dogs a day. While I was doing this story, he was discovered chewing on a boy's arm. The local residents were outraged but, like many people in Brasilia, Requenguela went unpunished. He has his four paws planted in the privilege of belonging to one of the most powerful men in Brasilândia.

Dona Elza, however, is not impressed by her potential son-in-law's protector or his sophisticated diet. She simply isn't keen on the relationship. She turned Fany into a canine Rapunzel, stationed atop the slab roof in full heat. Requenguela howled away below, his princely sword raised high. The street shook. But Dona Elza hadn't factored in the passion of her blazing red daughter. With no braids to let down, Fany threw her entire self off the roof—and landed with a swagger.

The second time, the outcome was more tragic. Banished to the slab on high, jumpy as a dog on a hot tin roof, Fany was frightened by something everyone else ignores: the fireworks announcing the arrival of a drug shipment to the favela. And she crashed down onto the sidewalk. They had to put pins in one of her hind legs. She's one of the latest victims of the drug trade, but she's recovering.

Dona Helena is one of the most no-nonsense women in Brasa. She has Japanese roots. She's been married for thirty-five years to João Ramos, a metalworker and a singer of Brazilian country-style *sertanejo* music, whenever possible and always more than his wife would like. Here is how things went: The matchmaker from the Japanese community arranged a candidate of nearly sixty for young Helena, then seventeen. While this was being cleared through her father, João invited some women workers from the purse factory to visit his mother in the cemetery. According to him, quite the date. It must have been, since the five women made a bet: whoever managed to snag João among the tombs wouldn't need to take her lunch box on Monday.

Dona Helena was the victor, but she got a lashing from her father. So João stole her away from home and carried her off to the other side of the hill. Her father died disillusioned. Brasilândia had not been kind to him. When he arrived, his name was Giro Nakamura; he became Júlio. His wife was Sizuko; they turned her into Aparecida. Their daughter Mariko Olena not only became Helena but also married João, who at night becomes João do Campo—Country John—to perform in a *sertanejo* duo with Oliveirinha.

But the most Shakespearean of Brasa's love stories doesn't involve people. The protagonist is a wiener dog named Paquito, who fell in love with the tire repairman's German shepherd. Talk about total anatomical incompatibility. "But talking did no good," says Tuca. "He'd cross Brasilândia to see the German shepherd." During one of these ventures into the impossible, Paquito was run over. "He died for love," everyone in Brasa says respectfully. The funeral, complete with a cross, drew one of the neighborhood's biggest crowds ever.

Out on the balcony, interrupted only by cars driving in from the city to pick up drugs on the hill, Dona Eugênia is full of sighs. Her melancholy ripples her silk dress. She would like to show me her wedding pictures, but her family was too poor for photographs. "My husband looked like Marcos Paulo," she says, referring to a soap opera star. "But you know, he never kissed me on the lips. And when he wanted me, he'd take me by force. Twenty-four years without a kiss." After her husband passed away, she met a colonel. She insisted on a "nice girl" courtship, and it was six months before she'd let him hold her hand. "That one, honey, kissed me even where he shouldn't. Only then did I learn about pleasure."

This time, Dona Eugênia isn't puffing away.

EVA AGAINST THE DEFORMED SOULS

This is the story of a woman who committed a crime that humanity will not forgive: she refused to be a victim. Eva Rodrigues met all the requirements for such a sentencing. She was a woman, poor thing. She was black, poor thing. She was poor, poor thing. Yet that wasn't all. Eva's birth had been a tough one and had left her with cerebral palsy. Her body trembled, she spilled her food, she had trouble walking. Everything about her was ungainly. The world reserved only one lot for Eva: being a poor thing. Eva could have reached out her hand to beg and would have received looks of profound pity. In exchange for some coins, she would have offered the donor not only the relief of charitable giving but also another, secret relief: the assurance that deformity, like madness, always lies in the Other.

Eva rebelled. She decided she wouldn't be a poor thing. Let the world deal with it. Let the world find other victims to satisfy its need to feel horror. This was Eva's crime, for which they never forgave her. Since no one could stamp the label "poor thing" on her forehead, they branded her with another. How could she, deformed, how could she, disabled, how could she, defective, dare reject the hand of charity, sister of pity and cousin of hypocrisy? How could she, abnormal, place herself on a par with those who are normal? It seemed as if the exhibition of Eva's twisted body revealed other people's twisted souls, as if Eva's exposed flaws laid bare other people's hidden flaws. How could Eva, *Eva* no less, dare to be imperfect in a world where fortunes are paid so that everyone is equally perfect? How could Eva dare to be different in a world where the equality of ideas is the only guarantee of safety? How could Eva dare win through her spirit in a world of appearances?

Oh, how pretentious Eva was. What grave danger Eva presented when she resolved not to be a poor thing. Eva went from victim to guilty as charged.

The story of how Eva revolted must be told, before revealing how they punished her. Eva doesn't know if it was the laughter that always hounded her, the imitations they did of her, or the announcement that it was her lot to stay crammed in a corner, preferably in silence. She only knows she decided that she wouldn't bow down, that she would reinvent her destiny. Reinvent herself.

Her first act of rebellion was to enroll in school. She accomplished this when she was nine, in the place where she was born, Restinga Seca, in central Rio Grande do Sul. Her hands wouldn't obey her. They were two agitated limbs that Eva didn't control. Eva used all the strength she possessed to get her left hand to hold her right. With one hand contorted over the other, in terrible pain from the effort, Eva wrote for the first time. The friction of hand bent over paper left her fingers raw. Her first notebooks contained bloodied letters, wounded words. Eva's first notebooks were written in blood.

Then Eva realized she was capable of rewriting her own destiny. And right from her first act of boldness, she received her first punishment. Even with top grades, she had to repeat the year. The teacher couldn't accept, couldn't understand, that Eva was able to write. Eva repeated the year and vowed she would repeat it as often as necessary until the teacher, until the world, understood that she would never give up; that she would prevail, even if it was by wearing them out; that they could ask everything of her, except the impossible—that they could ask everything of her, except that she stay in her place.

Eva soon learned that independence is quicksand, territory to be conquered and reconquered day after day. At the age of seventeen, in front of her eight siblings and her illiterate parents, landless farmers, she raised her first cry: "Enough! I'm not poor this, poor that. If I spill food when I'm eating, let me spill it. If I tip things over when I reach for them, let me tip them over. If I fall down, let me get up myself."

Eva moved to Porto Alegre. She got a job as a housemaid and finished junior high school. Her hands, like her soul, had been ulcerated by scars. But they no longer bled.

Eva enrolled at college, but couldn't afford it. They turned down her requests for student loans twice. She asked to transfer to a cheaper school. Eva dreamed of being a teacher. She wanted to teach how it is possible to write with festering hands, and to transform twisted hands into wings. But the disfigured souls who positioned themselves between Eva and the world were many. The fight had only just begun and would probably never end.

She heard it over and over: How can you write on the blackboard, shaking like that? How are you going to teach with such ugly handwriting? Don't you see you'll only be a bother? Don't you understand that between you and a normal girl, they'll pick the normal one? What do you want? Are you going to spend your life staring at a diploma on the wall? Eva heard all this from a teacher. Eva heard all this at college, proving that ignorance is to be found where you least expect it. Eva, the physically damaged, answered the damaged soul: "First of all, I'm not going to give up. Second, life is a risk. Not just for me. But for everyone."

It took Eva a while to realize why those intrepid creatures felt threatened by her shaking, how her frailty offended them. She was vilified in every known way and in some other ways invented just for her. First, they kept her from practice teaching. Then she was allowed to practice teach only at a school for the handicapped. Next, they decided she had to do it during the day, because they knew that was when she worked to pay her bills. Finally, since Eva would not give up, they gave up trying to impede her.

When Eva's name was pronounced at graduation, everyone stood, shouted, and clapped. Eva did not hear them. All of her senses were concentrated on not falling. Crossing the stage without tripping was the metaphor of her life. Eva would not fall, not there. And Eva didn't.

She was finally able to enter a classroom as a teacher. She was employed by at least three schools, and something happened at each. When they learned that Eva was not a poor thing, that hiring her was not an act of charity, everything changed. When they learned that Eva was capable, that you had to compete with her mind, not with her trembling, everything shifted. Initial commiseration transfigured into hatred. Who does this cripple think she is? That is what Eva heard, but didn't listen to. And so she was cast out of the world she had barely touched.

Eva didn't give up, and she won't. In 1994, she took a civil service exam for court page at the former appellate court. She thought the blindfolded eyes of Justice would not judge her for her deformity. She took the test in a special room for persons with disabilities. She passed in ninth place. Her appointment was posted in the official press. But, what do you know, Eva was rejected by the neurologist, because her hands shook, because she would drop the coffee tray.

A signature closed this chapter of a life. Eva went to court. The public defender didn't show up at trial, alleging she hadn't been informed. Eva pressed on. The suit is now before Brazil's Supreme Court. Eva went back to working as a housemaid.

Eva is a woman, poor and black. Eva's hands shake. All this they can accept. What they cannot forgive is that she refused to be a poor thing. What they cannot forgive Eva is that, as a poor black woman with a disability, she finished college—and in Brazil. All the cards were stacked against her and yet Eva dared to win the bet. This is why they revile her. Pay heed to Eva's words:

"Every time they knock me down, I'll get back up stronger. I won't hear of defeat. Defeat has never been in my plans. And 'poor things' are the ones who call me that."

Life abounds with paradoxes. Eva's is that people hate her because they cannot pity her. And the world's paradox is that the worst deformities are the invisible ones.

IN DEMON ZÉ'S BRAZIL

In Eldorado do Juma, site of Brazil's biggest gold rush since Serra Pelada, the boss is known as Demon Zé, though he's always talking about God. One of the men most blessed by this ore is a believer called "Got It," who believes he's a victim of the devil. In the town of Apuí, the mayor rails against gold prospecting, while the deputy mayor has abandoned city hall and amassed more than two kilos of gold, with both feet jammed in the mud. Bargeman Zé and Mariano hit the mother lode, but were driven off it by the barrel of a shotgun. The local church has been drained of its faithful, and the most distinguished lady in town auctioned off some girls when she inaugurated her cabaret. Here on the banks of the Juma River, the prostitutes charge in golden grams, yet they feel pleasure and even fall in love. This might sound like a magical realist novel, but it's all real. And it's happening now in the southern part of Amazonas state.

This tale of God and the devil began unfolding in the muggy 100-degree-Fahrenheit heat of the Amazon winter in December 2006, 285 miles from Manaus, and nearly 50 miles from Apuí, a town with a population of under twenty thousand carved out on the edge of the Trans-Amazonian Highway in the 1980s by Brazil's National Land Reform and Settlement Institute. Every day, pickup trucks, buses, motorcycles, and boats vomit out dozens of Brazilians, who arrive here from all folds of the map. They form ranks in a parking lot of mud where the gatekeeper of hell is a minister of God.

With a thundering German accent and revivalist's voice, Pastor Hains Hattge, of the Evangelical Congregational Church, charges ten dollars to park a car and five for a motorcycle. He is a creator of churches, as he introduces himself, who is now devoted to "privatizing" access to the gold fields while he searches for new deposits. "God writes right with crooked lines," he assures me.

The riverbank is lined with close to thirty *voadeiras*, the fastest motorboat in the Amazon. For another ten dollars per person and thirty minutes on the water, you can reach the left bank of the Juma River and the *corrutela*, the settlement that has grown up around the mines. It is a blend of medieval market and Wild West town, where gold or money can buy anything. Including .38-caliber bullets.

At first glance, the gold fields evoke scenes of biblical martyrdom. Tons of mud, resistant viruses, contaminated water, and the smell of human feces forced upon a brutalized slice of the jungle. Less than three months ago, this was virgin rainforest. Now it's a crater. At the bottom, fifty thousand men with fever in their eyes, their legs mired in clay, wrench gold from the bowels of the earth the old-fashioned way, by hand, because heavy machinery is prohibited. Like all informal mining sites, or *garimpos*, Eldorado do Juma is a cauldron where human passions combust. And they don't always smell good.

Nearly two dozen government security, mining, and environmental agencies have landed in the town of Apuí, intent on transforming Eldorado do Juma into a legal mining reserve. Before the gold rush, the National Land Reform and Settlement Institute held title to the land for settlement purposes. A prospectors cooperative, in which each member can purchase $150 quotas and pay for them in six installments, is now being formed. To keep the *garimpo* free of corpses, eighty-eight troops from the Amazonas State Military Police and thirty-two federal police officers have been dispatched to the region.

No one knows how many kilograms of gold have been extracted from the land. Official estimates range from 200 kilos to over 1.5 metric tons, or $4 million to $30 million worth. Specialists wager that the real figure falls closer to the lower end. The first rule in the *garimpo* is to never tell the truth about quantities. Even if his mattress is stuffed with gold, a prospector will always swear on his life that he's down on his luck.

So far, Eldorado do Juma hasn't shown signs that it holds either the size or the amount of gold required to repeat the 1970s phenomenon of Serra Pelada. Whoever got here first occupied the land. Those arriving now are *rodado*, or "foundered," as they say of a laborer who has neither riches nor a job. But in the words of Louro, a prospector from Porto Velho, capital of the neighboring state of Rondônia, no dose of reality dilutes "the gold virus inoculated into the blood." "We can pretend we're something else, do other jobs, until a new strike comes along," he says. "But it's enough to hear the call, and even if he's got a good job, a guy drops everything and hits the road with the clothes on his back. A prospector is a hopeful kind of guy."

Bargeman Zé and Mariano: The First War

From sunup to sundown, thousands of men claw into the dirt in search of high-quality gold, 98 percent pure. At a jewelry shop, eighteen-karat gold is only 75 percent pure. To reach the mother lode, you must advance some two miles along trails cut into the bush, through mud, filthy water, and mining pits. There beats the heart of the *garimpo*. But the sound of its pulse is the roar of chainsaws toppling centuries-old trees, and, in the days before the police arrived, of gunshots.

In early 2006, four workhands named Agenor, Neguinho, Paulo, and Tibúrcio were setting up a farm in the forest when they spied gold glittering. They grubbed it up bit by bit, on the sly. But late that year, one of them drenched his tongue in *cachaça* at a bar in Apuí, and word spread—the word being *fofoca*, which refers both to the news of gold and to its whereabouts. "I'm riding on top of gold," he supposedly said. His breach of trust echoed through hearts and minds, and there were many who swept the forest to stalk down any ore in the vicinity. Whenever there's an announcement like this, a horde of hopefuls vanishes into the forest.

Bargeman Zé and Mariano are "seasoned," as they call the prospectors who have the gold bug churning in their veins alongside leukocytes and hemoglobin. The two men trembled at the news of the *fofoca*. It was in November 2006, and Mariano was hanging out at a bar in Apuí. His footsteps were intercepted by his old buddy, Bargeman Zé: "Mariano, let's open a hole?" Right away.

Two miles from the old *garimpo*, Mariano, a man whose eyes bulge from all the world he has beheld, discovered where the gold was sparkling. "With the grace of God," he says. "Gold that's going to yield three hundred, four hundred grams a day." Then his back gave out and he had to emerge from the forest to seek help. Bargeman Zé was left on his own. "About twelve men armed with pistols, rifles, and shotguns surrounded me," he says. "I didn't have a chance. They forced me to show them the mother lode." These two frontiersmen were left with a less golden piece of this *fofoca* that inflames Brazil and with the torture of watching others strike it rich, pulling from the earth enough gold to change a life.

Bargeman Zé is missing some teeth but doesn't miss out on a chance to laugh. "We're used to not having much. We resign ourselves," he says. Mariano seems like a man who hasn't withered away only because his very anger keeps him on track. "I've been looking for a strike like this since I was eighteen. I just got here and started losing. I feel like I've got a screw squeezing my heart."

In the brutal way things get done on this side of the world, Bargeman Zé and Mariano had learned they'd invaded Demon Zé's land.

A Boss Named after the Devil

Once the gold had glittered on the town's website, the news swept the world. Eldorado do Juma is Brazil's first case of a digital *fofoca*, and so the rush got off to a fast start. In the second half of December 2006, the phone rang in a "not so nice" house in São Miguel do Guaporé, in Rondônia: "Zé, your lands have been invaded by prospectors." He mounted a vehicle.

Demon Zé's name calls to mind a hired gun who has made a pact with the devil. Nope. In flesh and blood, Demon Zé is more like a drudge laborer than a landowner. Shaped by the wrangling of steers, his body carries a complete canvas of Brazilian woes. Just like his land deed, which the National Land Reform and Settlement Institute says is worth as much as a bingo card.

Demon Zé unfolds the deed carefully, showing a respect only the illiterate have for written things. The contract was drawn up in the forest on June 5, 2004, in blue ink on a page torn from a notebook. "The three of us were in the forest. Only Donizette knew how to write. He did it for me," he says. The paper states that "Sebastião Matias de Carvalho aka Santos" sold José Ferreira da Silva Filho, Demon Zé's official name, "a section of land measuring 6,200 across, on the left bank of the Juma River." Payment was an "XR

200 motorcycle, year 2001, color black, worth one thousand dollars." So it was, in this stumbling way, that Demon Zé bought a golden piece of the Amazon.

As the *patrão*, or boss, of the *garimpo*, Demon Zé has been demanding 8 percent of all the gold found in the pits on his land until such time as the cooperative defines another form of operation. In terms of its hierarchy and network of obligations, the *garimpo* seems to draw inspiration from feudalism, with its overlords, vassals, and serfs. Whoever got here first, or had more armed men to steal from whoever got here first, staked out a large chunk of a pit to work. It falls to these headmen to settle up with Demon Zé.

To secure ownership, the headmen assign a few dozen men to plow up their claims. Like nobility, the headmen don't stick their hands in the mud or pick up a shovel; they just manage, oversee, and guarantee security. Their men can lease out part of the land and make similar arrangements with their own laborers, or operate on shares: 50 percent for the headman, 50 percent for the worker. This is the most common system. There are day workers as well, at two grams a day, with one gram worth twenty dollars. And, at the poorest base of the gold laborer's pyramid, come the *requeiros*, the "supplicants," who roam the mines, gold-pans in hand, asking permission to try their luck in the gravel that the "legitimate" owners have already sifted through.

In actuality, the headmen have more power than Demon Zé himself, because they have better control over the gold and more men to enforce their will. They're like aristocrats in some periods of the Middle Ages who had their own armies, wielded more authority than their king—and could even defy him. This is the production system the Brazilian government is trying to change by setting up a co-op. But for now, the world is still spinning the same old way in Eldorado do Juma.

A Certain "Little Saint" César

Everyone who comes to the *garimpo* is indoctrinated to believe that Demon Zé is the almighty above the gold. But while his name was reverberating over the Juma like a threat from the netherworlds, here was how things were actually going for the man who bears Beelzebub's name: he was locked up in a hotel room in downtown Apuí by order of his manager, Humberto César de Andrade Reis, who had Zé on such a short leash that he could go out only to take his meals. "César said that they wanted to kill me in the *garimpo*, that I couldn't show my face," says Demon Zé.

César showed up on the banks of the Juma as if out of nowhere, gold chain round his neck and safari jacket on his back. He claimed he was with the "Federals." According to the police, he ran off in late January with "$12,500 to $15,000 and more than three kilos of Demon Zé's gold." Zé the boss was left with $40,000 and a pickup purchased on credit. "That's Little Saint César," jokes Antônio José Ribeiro Nunes, a mining engineer with Brazil's national mining agency.

Some weeks later, Demon Zé the miner tells his story in a cheap hotel in downtown Manaus, where he has come to sort out some papers he is unable to decipher. He feels cornered in the big city, and ashamed that he doesn't know how to fill out the hotel registration form. When he starts talking, he cries. "They call me Demon Zé because there's never been an unbroken beast I couldn't tame, ever since I was little. I've been driving cattle since I was eight, and at that age I vowed to Our Lady of Aparecida that one day I'd have my own home. Before this *garimpo*, I had never put my hands on more than $2,500 of my own money, only the rancher's, to pay some bill. My parents registered me when I was fifteen, till then I didn't even exist. I put on my first shoes when I was sixteen, because my feet were so hobbled by the stones of Goiás that I couldn't stand to walk anymore. I bought them on credit at the shop of some guy called Vanicó, Conga sneakers, the kind with white rubber toes."

Up until then, Demon Zé's only gold had been a tooth at the gateway to his mouth. "I was still young and embarrassed to have one tooth riding on top of the other. So I planted some black beans, harvested them, and gave them to the dentist so he could put this tooth in. The others started hurting and I kept having them pulled. Now, if the gold holds out, I'm going to get all my teeth fixed." If his deed is worthless, his request for a mining permit from the government agency is legit. He has priority mining rights. This is why Demon Zé hasn't been erased from the ferocious war in the *garimpo*.

Just to be safe, Demon Zé keeps a little medal of Our Lady of Aparecida dangling from his brown hat. When he walks around Apuí, a bodyguard named Salomão Cícero, an officer with the military police, trails behind. Corporal Cícero defines his boss this way: "Mr. Demon hasn't been to school, he's a real simple man. He doesn't have difficulties, he has 'diffu-kil-ties.' But he's a good man and he's going to give me a little something."

Got It and the Gold of the Faithful

Got It is one of the headmen who make up the nobility of Eldorado do Juma. His story is an Amazonian folly. By the age of thirty-seven, four kids, he had led a life of so many tribulations that even the minister at the Assembly of God sometimes thinks it is too much for one mortal. Here's the short version of his story: Years ago a heavy door crashed down on Got It's head and a blood clot in his brain left him stuck in a wheelchair. Dumper Blackie, also born-again, carried him on his back to a healing service. "God worked a miracle in him," Pastor Fernandes says.

They say Got It left the church on his own two feet, strong enough to get up at 5:00 a.m. and start pushing the cart that baptized him in the city: "I got it! Got what? I got sweet rolls, I got coffee cake, got homemade bread, sandwich bread, bread rolls." And then chicken fritters, rissole, juice, and yogurt. Got It made fifty dollars a month wheeling around town. When he had two abdominal hernias operated on, he couldn't wait out the recovery period because his kids didn't have shoes to wear to school. He went back to the streets before his stitches were healed, and they went bad inside him.

On the night of December 17, 2006, Got It was one of the most battered souls in Apuí—and the competition is decidedly fierce. He had sold his cart and few belongings and went to track down treatment in Porto Velho. He says God sent him a dream in the middle of the night, where he saw himself in a mining pit. Got It sat up in bed and told his wife, Dona Milca, that he had changed courses. Slashing his way through the forest, he eventually came to perch at the top of a mining pit that proved to hold the mother lode. In the first two weeks of January, Got It became Danildo da Silva for the first time.

Now he was a man "kilo-ed" in gold. Even the deputy mayor, Aminadal de Souza, went to ask him for a stretch of land to work. "That guy had never given me the time of day. I told him the truth: I'm going to put priority on the meek," says Got It. "The deputy mayor bowed his head and was gone."

Next, a thriving businessman from Apuí got stuck in the mud to offer him a deal: he would pay Got It the city price for gold in exchange for the right to be the exclusive supplier of goods in his piece of the *garimpo*. But Got It remembered he'd once gone with Dona Milca to buy a mattress, money all counted out in his pocket so he could pay cash, and the merchant had gotten snooty: "You can only buy with a credit card or guaranteed check here." With this memory still throbbing in his head, Got It declined the offer: "And just look, I still don't have a credit card or guaranteed check." Those were three glorious weeks. With all his God-fearing humility, Got It showed that the world goes round.

Unfortunately for him, it does indeed go round. When Dumper Blackie roared in from the *garimpo* on his motorcycle "at seventy-five miles an hour, bag slung over his shoulder," thinking he was the singer Roberto Carlos on the winding Santos highway, the strap tore. "The mayonnaise jar holding three kilos of Got It's gold broke," says Blackie. Sixty thousand dollars' worth. He puts a look of compunction on his round face to lend the tale greater credence: "It left a 150-foot trail of gold. I picked up what I could."

On Sunday, January 21, the police went to the *garimpo* to get Got It. The safe at the hardware store owned by José Ribeiro, the third born-again in this story, had been busted open with a pickax. Guess what they took. Yes, of course, Got It's gold. "They made off with his two and a half kilos of gold, plus 950 grams of mine and $6,500 in cash from the house I'd sold to pay off some debts," says Ribeiro. "I'm God-fearing, but if I had had a gun, nobody would've gotten out of there alive."

That night, Got It, Dumper Blackie, and Ribeiro cried in each other's arms at the Assembly of God church. The pastor evoked Job and wore himself ragged explaining that the gold had been "the sovereign will of God" and the robbery had been "the permissive will of God." The following Tuesday, Got It spent six hours at the hospital. On Wednesday, he was ready to pick life back up again, start his own business, and, as soon as possible, realize the dearest dream of Dona Milca, his twenty-four-year-old born-again wife, who is taking high school equivalency classes. What is the long-haired, bare-foot girl's dream? "I want to visit the Museum of the Portuguese Language in São Paulo. I saw a program on TV, and I thought the shaping of the words was real pretty."

When goodbyes are said, Got It informs me the devil isn't going to laugh in his face this time around. In a low voice, almost a whisper, Got It says . . . he's still got it.

The Mayor, the Priest, and Francisco's Two Sons

In Apuí, only two prominent figures argue aloud that gold has been a rotten deal for the town. One is the mayor, Antônio Roque Longo, a diligent man of brief stature, despite his last name. He dreads the day when the foundered people from the *garimpo* show up at city hall seeking help. "Those people there are living in subhuman conditions. We're going to have a social problem on our hands soon," he predicts. And he suffers. The other local opponent is Friar Itacir Fontana, who even called up the public radio station and tried to convince them to declare over the air that the gold rush is a sham. "They kept passing me back and forth on the line," he grumbles. He suffers, too.

The mayor had the displeasure of seeing his deputy, Aminadal de Souza, head into the *garimpo*, gold-panning kit in hand, completely unabashed. The two don't get along. They don't even speak. Aminadal became known as the "deputy miner" in the fields. He sold a 1994 pickup, bought the right to mine a pit, and made two and a half kilos of gold in fifteen days. What for? "To buy another pickup," he explains. "Red."

Friar Itacir has tallied a list of churchgoers who are in sin. Mass is half-empty. The church pews hold only women. The clergyman had to cancel the luncheon honoring the patron saint, Saint Sebastian, for lack of a quorum. The festival's cattle auction flopped for the same reason. Bearded, wearing a gray robe, Friar Itacir refuses to lasso his stray lambs by the ears. "Doesn't do any good. My sheep are grazing in other pastures now, my dear. You can offer them the best feed, but it doesn't do any good. Now it's just gold. Gold and more gold."

Hell depends a lot on how much of heaven you know. "The *garimpo* is a blessing from God," Telmo Torraca shouts from under his black plastic tarp. "Look what the *garimpo* does to a man. You bring down trees, get stuck in the mud. But when I put my eyes on the forty-five grams of gold that I got here in thirty days, all I could see was a couple of cows to give my old lady milk." His farm in Apuí has 140 acres of weak soil. "But it's mine," he says. He named his farmstead New Heaven and New Earth. A place that harbors all of a man's hopes, he believes, rightfully deserves a pair of cows paid for in their weight in gold.

For these many reasons, the mayor and the priest are two leaders completely alone. It's not only the poor, faithful voters who have followed the gleam of gold. Throwing themselves into it body and soul, the elite of Apuí have overcome one or another qualm of a moral nature and endeavored to secure the biggest share of the none-too-base metal in their own hands. Not only do they sell merchandise to the miners—some have set up a prospecting consortium at $2,000 per quota to explore the still-virgin forest for the most exclusive gold deposits.

It should be made clear that the cream of Apuí society is composed of bold, adventuresome people who left their home states in pursuit of land and opportunity in northern Brazil, and here they settled. "I came here after I saw that movie *Bye Bye Brazil*," says shop owner Francisco Soares Neto. "I was born under the rule of the big honchos in Alagoas, and my father sent me away before I could lock horns with that system. I tried Rio, I tried São Paulo. Then I saw that long road in *Bye Bye Brazil* and thought this was the last place in my country without an owner. I came here, settled in, and now I'm putting two through college."

Francisco is talking about his sons, to whom he gave names that prophesy the future he has traced out for them: "Melchizedek means one who has no roots, who isn't something because of his birthplace but because of who he is. And Jeftomar was a brawling captain in the Egyptian army. A fighter. It's all there, in the Bible." Francisco had to make a hurried trip from Apuí to São Paulo to stock up on cleats, Tactel shorts, and other *garimpo* favorites. "I'm selling them for triple," he gloats.

Dona Andréia's Cabaret and the Saga of the Hookers Who Come

There are no limits to the entrepreneurial spirit that seeks to wrest from the prospectors the gold that they wrest from the earth. "I'm a cattle drover who mines miners," explains Nilberto Leite, a vendor who works out of the mining settlement. He sells $2,000 in goods a day to the big guys, besides two or three head of cattle. Plus the gold he buys at $18 a gram, worth $20 in the city.

But when it comes to spunk, nobody outdoes the entrepreneur Andréia Gobbi, a striking woman of thirty-four with three rosy kids and keen business acumen. Before the gold appeared, she and her husband ran the biggest supermarket in Apuí. "Then I had an idea. I went to visit the *garimpo* and noticed they didn't have any entertainment there," the businesswoman says. "I thought, 'There's a little money to be made here.'" Keeping it all in the family, she put the idea to her twenty-year-old brother, Marcos Rafael Bom, who withdrew from veterinary school in the southern state of Paraná and moved to Apuí with his girlfriend, Vanessa.

Thus was born Andressa's Night Club, an amalgam of the two businesswomen's names. It stands right across from the mining village, of course, but on the other side of the river to circumvent the police-imposed curfew that shuts night down at 10:00 p.m. Twenty-five young girls, chosen in Manaus, will brighten the club's grand opening, featuring music and striptease, and twenty rooms at four grams each, paid for by whichever young woman takes advantage of it. "We're going to start by auctioning off the ten prettiest," pro-claims Marcos. "And we're going to make a lot of gold."

Doraci dos Santos Silva, or Dora, and Elisângela Pereira da Costa aren't gals for an auction. First of all, because they're over twenty and their bellies have rounded out from giving birth (Dora three, Elisângela four). But mainly because their thing is turning their bodies into independent microbusinesses. Dora and Elisângela are no easy pickings for a pimp, much less a madam. They walked into the *garimpo* with spice in their sway and a plan in their heads. "Where there's a *fofoca*, there I go. I brought some costume jew-elry with me to sell and six boxes of condoms," says Dora. "The brand name ones are for me, the counterfeit ones I sell."

Thirty-year-old Dora, more *garimpos* on her résumé than years of life, leaves her children with her mother and goes from mining town to mining town, stashing away money so she can open a diner. A prospector put a first baby in her belly when she was fifteen. Then the same gent fathered another two besides. Before hitting the road and landing in Eldorado do Juma, she got a letter from him, post-marked in the state of Roraima, asking her to marry him. Dora didn't falter. Before taking off, she mailed a reply demanding a photo. "First I need to see what he looks like today," she explains.

Elisângela had a husband until a little while ago. But the guy went out to buy meat when she was expecting her third child and hours later came back drunk. He hit her three times across the face and slammed her against the wall. Her seven-month belly didn't get in the way. Elisângela grabbed a stick and kicked the scourge out. "Can you believe that man went to complain to the police cap-tain?" she says. "I was left with two kids, had the third alone, and he even came back to make the fourth."

If a hooker in the *garimpo* knows what she's doing, she com-mands respect, enjoys status, walks with her head high. Business relations here bear no resemblance to trick-turning in the city. There are few women for many needy men. Beneath a black tarp or a starry sky, sex is coy, with ambitions of romance. When the women show up on the riverbank, lipstick applied, fragrance in their hair, they first hunt down a job as a cook. They are paid thirty grams of gold a month to serve up food for the gang.

While these women turn a trick here and there, charging around four to five grams, or eighty to a hundred dollars, they set about selecting a man for his skill in digging gold from the earth and not spending it all on gambling and drinking. Then they enter into a temporary matrimonial arrangement. They are considered the mistress of one man only, who supports them and their kids back in the city. Their cook's wages go straight into the piggy bank, free from expenses. As an added bonus, nobody messes with them. In the *garimpo*, a kept woman has the caliber of a wife. Lay a hand on her, take a bullet.

The plan is perfect, but since "perfection is only found in matters of God," there's always a flaw. Dora and Elisângela sigh in unison. Because there are handsome men in the *garimpo* too, men with bedroom eyes, bodies sculpted from so much wrestling with gold, sweet-talking as *pagode* singers. "Our trouble is that when we fall in love, we end up with some good-for-nothing who louses up our lives. Then we're out of luck," says Dora sadly. "There's some lady-killers who drive you wild in bed, take a woman where her husband never did, make her come," says Elisângela, both ruing and wanting.

The two women try to knock sense into each other so this tragedy won't befall them at Eldorado do Juma. But the next day, one of them is seen sneaking around with a dark-skinned, cat-eyed fellow who looks like he has nowhere for his equilibrist body to call home.

A Saga of Wayfaring Brazilians

At first glance, the only thing that appears is the gigantic gash torn in the belly of the forest by human hands. But the saga unfolding in southern Amazonas today means much more. Here lies the Brazil that journeys. Eldorado do Juma is merely the latest stop for these people before they set off in pursuit of a new promise. These are people who sometimes walk barefoot, willing to die with their nails dug into the ground if need be, but searching for a place they have yet to find in Brazil. They sell everything but never the essential: a restless, desirous soul that has them yearning for a way to snare a patch of land, a better house, a used car, or just some hope clutching the wind so the dream can go on. That's not little. "People like us, doesn't matter where we are, miss, we're always in the hollow of Brazil," says Got It.

Mamédio Chagas de Oliveira has little schooling but knows his numbers as fits his needs. He's what they call a supplicant, floundering in the mud and the social pyramid of the gold fields. Taking up his pan, he sifts gently through the gravel to see if it still glitters where others have given up. "I got four grams of gold one day and five the next. In two days I made what I make in a month selling rugs around the streets of Manaus," he says. "It's simple. If I had a good life, I wouldn't be here buried in mud."

Elias Simão, forty-four long-suffering years old, lies in a hospital bed in Apuí. He spent only two weeks as an "unbroken" prospector, the term for a novice in the trade. Enough for his soul to fill up with this breath, and his body to be immediately destroyed, afflicted by pneumonia and an intestinal infection. Does he regret it?

With a seasoned smile, he declares: "No. It's left me happy. You know, since I was little, I've known nothing but farm fields. Even my cradle was a field. Coffee, rice, black beans, corn, chickens, pigs. If it wasn't for the *garimpo*, even my casket would be a field. I learned something new there. I'm going back to cropping, but now I've got this adventure inside me." He proudly taps his back pocket using the hand not tied to the IV: "Part of the fifteen grams that I got is here in my pocket."

Astride the trunk of a newly dead tree, a boy ignores the stench of human feces plaguing the air and opens his mouth wide in introduction. His is one of the few smiles that merit the adjective "twenty-four-karat." Five diamonds are embedded in his decaying teeth. "I brought them from the Roosevelt *garimpo*, from the land of the Cinta-Larga," says Daniel Guilhermino da Silva. He doesn't have even fifteen dollars in his pocket, much less thirty grams of gold. But a stretch of the map has traveled aboard this poor man's body. His mouth carries not only all his assets but also his essence. "I love this mud, this ruckus, these crowds. Isn't it nice?" he says. And off he goes.

ADAIL WANTS TO FLY

His name is Adail José da Silva, and he lives at the gate to heaven, where the state of Rio Grande do Sul soars off into the world and where the world sets down in Rio Grande do Sul. Thirty-six years ago, he disembarked here, at the entrance to Porto Alegre's Salgado Filho Airport. He felt the differences early on, during his jumbled landing. He arrived in a weary-springed bus that emerged from the mountains of his birthplace, where his hands had been stained by the blood of pine forests. Adail arrived scared to death, because the only plane he had ever seen in his life had smashed into the hills in the town of Canela, a fallen bird that for weeks mesmerized a legion of people from the countryside who flew solely with both feet on the ground. He arrived with his red leather suitcase clutched to his body, half a dozen personal odds and ends inside. At the main door of the airport—only half the size it is today, but enormous to him—he pulled up short, and refused to enter.

His friends pushed him, and Adail stumbled his way in, holding his awkward suitcase but no plane ticket. At the dawn of that October in 1963, a journey began that never got off the ground and that still continues today. Adail became what he would be for the rest his life. He became the baggage-handling "boy," and thus discovered the relativity of distance, because he was so near and yet always so far. He was fewer than one hundred steps from the wings of a plane, but could never reach them.

All that was left for Adail was to love the winged profiles of his fate from afar. He who had never, from his first day, understood how those uproaring things could fly. So much metal, so many people, so many suitcases. Good lord, how was it possible? As he stuffed the bellies of those steel birds, Adail saw the world rush by, coming and going at a frightening pace. He wanted to be the baggage engorging the plane. He saw all of Brazil's presidents, from João Goulart to Fernando Henrique Cardoso. He saw Pelé and the singer Roberto Carlos. He grew old with Tônia Carrero, carrying the luggage of the actress he still considers the most beautiful woman in Brazil.

Adail saw the world, but the world didn't always see Adail. The world changed and Adail changed. But neither changed enough to shrink the distance between the porter and the plane. Because, at the age of sixty-two, Adail is still what his clients shout from the arrivals door: "Hey, boy!" And the world still belongs to these clients. But Adail, oh Adail—Adail hasn't given up on flying.

"You didn't want to work at the airport at first. Why not?"

"I thought it wasn't a man's job. I spent over a year hiding at the airport. Then I got used to being a bum."

"Is it worth it, living close to airplanes?"

"I built a house that's not much but it's mine. I raised three kids . . . all based on aviation. To me, aviation fell out of heaven!"

"What's annoying about this life?"

"I get annoyed when those show-offs go to the United States and come back bad-mouthing Brazil. Those guys are brownnosers, right? Because I've never been anywhere else, but I know there's no country better than Brazil. I haven't been, but I hear all the talk at the airport. The United States might be loaded with democracy, but take a look how they treat their black people there, just look."

"What do your clients call you?"

"The *doutores* call me like this: 'Hey, boy!' I think it's actually affectionate."

"And you call them doctor?"

"To me, they're all *doutores*. Fellow gets off at the airport, he's a *doutor*. So I say, 'Hello, *doutor*.' 'How's it going, *doutor*?' 'Right away, *doutor*.'"

"Is that the secret to your job?"

"You've got to be humble. No good being arrogant. Because if I was a big shot, I wouldn't be carrying other people's suitcases, right? I'm just a nobody. So I've got to put myself in my place."

"What's the farthest you've been in your life?"

"Criciúma. My neighbor took me there to buy clothes. I got to the border and said, 'Wow, I've left Brazil!'"

"What's the nicest thing about airplanes?"

"Takeoff. Whenever I can, I go up top and take a peek. I still haven't figured them out. Seems like they're not going to get off the ground, then they lift up and look like a bird. A vulture."

"Would you like to fly?"

"It's my dream. But I've lost hope. Poor people don't fly."

"Where would you like to fly to?"

"To the Shrine of Our Lady of Aparecida, to fulfill a vow. Fifteen years back I promised I'd go there if Our Lady healed my legs. I'd almost quit walking. She healed me. I tried to go with my wife, Maria Cedir, but I couldn't even afford the bus."

"What did you promise the saint?"

"I've got to put a pair of my socks on the altar there."

"What do you think it's like to fly?"

"It must be really fun. I see that wide world of people all happy. That flying stuff just has to be good!"

"What do you think it's like?"

"I don't even know how you're supposed to act inside a monster like that. Do you know if they usher people to their seats?"

"Tell me about your dream."

"I'd like to go on a DC-10, the great biggest of them all. And on the mightiest, on Varig airlines. I've got an old suit I'd send off to the cleaners and I'd sit in first class. With all my just deserves. Where there's no waiting, just wallowing. And I'd do like the *doutores*. I'd get there and say [*imitating them, Adail juts out his chin and projects his voice*]: 'First class!'"

"And then?"

"Then I'd sit there like a shark, and smoke a nice fine cigar. Then I'd motion to the stewardess—'Give me some of that fancy Scotch.' Then I'd have it all. There'd be nothing missing in my life."

"What would you eat?"

"Eat? Do you have to eat? I don't think I'd eat. I'm used to my beans and rice at home. But if I could ask for anything, well then I'd ask for a little shrimp."

"Do you like shrimp?"

"Never had it. I'd like to know what it's like."

"And on your return?"

"I'd go back to my hometown and tell my relatives, 'I've flown on a plane.'"

"What suitcase would you take?"

"You know, I don't have one. To ride on a plane, I'd buy one of those with wheels. I think they're nifty."

"Who'd carry it for you?"

"Oh, the Kraut! He's real stuck-up. I'd give him five bucks and tell him to carry the boy's suitcase."

"What will it be like, the day you fly?"

"It'll be the day the guys at the airport say: 'Here comes Dr. Adail!' On that day at least, I'll be the *doutor*."

THE MAN WHO EATS GLASS

From inside a circle made of shards of glass in front of Porto Alegre's Public Market, a scrawny man, little more than a twig of skin, fired a bottomless question at me point blank:

"Miss, tell me something. Do you think I should keep on eating glass or give it up, go back home, and put in some crops?"

I remained stock-still, not knowing what to say, utterly mute. Should he continue eating glass or not? It was a question and a half. Then I understood. Jorge Luiz Santos de Oliveira, thus christened thirty-five years ago, had a dream, the dream of making a living by eating glass. Because eating glass is Jorge Luiz's art. From early on, it was what set Jorge Luiz apart from the sad hordes of all the Jorges, from the long line of country people from São Jerônimo, his land, coal land, dark and pungent. By masticating his rocky ground, Jorge Luiz discovered he is a unique being in the world, despite the sameness of his melancholy face, of skin stretched over bones. By gnawing on stones to frighten off the worms crawling around his insides, he blazed the trail of his art. For someone who regurgitated stones, glass wasn't scary.

Jorge Luiz began by ingesting beer, cognac, even champagne bottles. He became, in the words of his crude cardboard poster, the Man of Steel. And so, while ruminating on a liter bottle of Scotch—on the rocks—Jorge Luiz asked me this question from the fork in his path: Should he or should he not continue eating glass?

I moved closer to understand the question. Then I noticed. The Man of Steel was crying.

Jorge Luiz had no audience, inescapably a tragedy for a performer. He drew the traditional circle of water to summon his public, but they didn't come. They were all standing around an indigenous man displaying a lizard in a box and selling some miraculous ointments that, he guaranteed, came straight from the Amazon. Earlier, Jorge Luiz had tried to do his performance over at a busy pedestrian mall, but he left when he caught sight of the man who owns the spot, the magisterial Brazilian Rambo, with his admirable bundle of muscles.

So the Man of Steel hustled over to Glênio Peres Plaza with his many riches: a leather hat, a bag filled with pieces of glass, a photo of his two kids, and a note, written by him, in which he vows to love beyond this life the wife who was run over and killed two years ago. "Tatiane, Iloveyou," it reads, the words stuck together so he won't ever be separated from the woman of his life again, not even by the vacuum of grammar.

When I met him, Jorge Luiz had just shattered an eyetooth on a shard from an imported bottle of something he'd pulled out of a trash can. Tough glass, said the startled Man of Steel, a bright red thread trickling from the corner of his mouth. He told me his idol and inspiration was Ostrich Man, who had swallowed pool balls in his childhood, and padlocks too, keys and all, right down the hatch.

Now Jorge Luiz couldn't understand why people would rather watch a boring lizard do nothing at all than watch a man eat glass, lie down on glass, walk on glass. Nor could I. Strange world this, where a man eating glass isn't astonishing.

The two of us stood there, glaring at the lizard and pondering human mysteries. Then I left, without answering his question from the depths. He chewed glass but what pierced him was invisibility.

OLD FOLKS HOME

Suddenly they've arrived here, in front of the iron gate at the old people's home, their whole lives squeezed into a carry-on. They've left behind a vast web of delicate things, all those many decades of struggle between yearnings and possibilities. Their family, their furniture, their neighborhood, the cracks in the wall, a glass by the sink, the outline of their body on the mattress. Reduced to a single verb tense, the past, they have a questionable present and a future nobody wants.

They too thought old age would be someone else's fate. They never suspected they would stand before this gateway. At the threshold they discover that a single step is tantamount to crossing an abyss. They have been left here because other people decided their time was up. Cast into a house that isn't theirs, amid unfamiliar furniture, faces they don't recognize, and memories that don't fit, they are reduced to telling a story no one wants to hear because it lies in the past.

"I didn't want to say goodbye to my house," says Sandra Carvalho. "I just asked my son to bring me the cabinet with my knickknacks, the couch, my armchair, a table, and my photographs. Since then,

I've been living with what's left." Sandra came here with her ailing husband. He died eight months ago. Sandra stayed. Their grandchildren in the photos have grown, their children's eyes are colored with new nuances, their house has been rented out. Even the city has gained and lost. But Sandra didn't see this.

There's something tragic about the iron gate at the São Luiz Old Age Home. Better than most, the institution is clean and decent, with lots of warm touches. Like all other homes for the elderly, it will be their last address, a shelter invented to hide those who have no place in the world, trapped between the medical advances that have enabled them to get this far and a society that only values youth. The home is elderly as well, its 111 years of existence played out in the neighborhood of Caju, site of Rio de Janeiro's largest cemetery, the final destination for everyone there.

Viscount Ferreira D'Almeida, founder of the home and man of fervent faith, accompanies every step taken along the pathway of trees leading to the heart of the place. His bronze stare is omnipresent, keeping vigil over the 257 elderly who share this citadel divided into six towers, each christened in honor of a saint or one of the centuries-old Rio de Janeiro families that used to make hefty donations to guarantee a spot in heaven.

The sturdiness of the founder's statue notwithstanding, the home has changed over time. It was born before the invention of retirement for the purpose of housing laborers from the aristocrat's textile factories once they no longer had the strength to handle machinery. One century later, it is inhabited by former liberal professionals and merchants, entrepreneurs and intellectuals; by people from the middle class, as well as those with illustrious last names who can afford a private room.

Those who never managed to purchase a place all their own in the world occupy one of the forty free beds in an airy but collective ward. They were once laborers, shop clerks, seamstresses, washerwomen, maids. As on the outside, a long stairway lies between rich and poor. The beds that shelter slumber and fright are different.

Sandra Carvalho, mother of three, grandmother of six, and great-grandmother of two, is lucky enough to have her own room. Otherwise, there would be nothing but a wardrobe in which to store eighty years of life. Sandra arrived at the gate by the hands of her middle child. She wanted to live with him in the United States. Not possible. "It'd be real complicated," she persuades herself. "I wanted to be a singer, I was a seamstress. My life was always so filled with strife . . ." She caresses the smiles on the photos in her wedding album and murmurs, "I've faded away here. Yes, I've faded away."

Sandra, like all of them, is a victim of a corner of time. The elderly have lost bonds, friendship, and warmth, and gained years. They live longer than their parents and grandparents, and they live more alone. Social death arrives before their final heartbeat. Their pace becomes too slow for the speed of a world that doesn't forgive falling. They have become inconvenient evidence. The society that left them at the gate walks on murky ground. Not even by paying the price of the best plastic surgeon can youth be stretched out forever. Wrinkled, unsure, they are a bothersome reminder not of the past, but of everyone's future.

On the threshold of the home, they decide they want to live. They do so as far as possible, in part because they are old enough to understand that the possible is not trivial. In this place where the elderly are cut off from time, the world, and their families, they perform a daily encore of resistance and insurrection. They desire—a different flavor on the menu, a sexual fantasy about a muse now older than they are, tomorrow's newspaper. As long as they desire, even though they're cut off from the world, they'll be alive. Because, beyond the triumphs of science, living is more than breathing.

At the age of seventy-four, Fermelinda Paes Campos, a Portuguese-born retired merchant, fulfills a rite of rebellion every day by dressing up for a party. She drapes herself in pearls and diaphanous fabric. "These hormones won't leave me alone. I'm exploding," she confides. Stuck in a wheelchair, former journalist Paulo Serrado, seventy-one, dreams he is mounted on an eagle, riding over mountains. "I wake up feeling like a fool, but that's all right." Now unable to dance, he was once known as Fred Astaire by Copacabana's bohemian crowd. Holding tight to Cyd Charisse's portrait—"the loveliest legs in film"—he twirls around in his fantasies. Eighty-nine-year-old Rosa Bela Ohanian lived in Europe and the United States, served on the diplomatic staff in Washington, and speaks four languages. She emerges from her melancholy to croon a love song in Danish: "I love a whole lifetime, not just a moment."

Near the end, life becomes a movie where you would like to add characters, cut scenes, liven up the colors in the photography. Or replace the sound track of elevator music with some heavy metal, or a tango by Piazzolla. At eighty-six, Guilherme Coelho, once a construction foreman, prefers to dwell in regret. He rues how he wallowed in the flesh when he was young. Now he is wholly transformed into spirit, a Bible within reach. He spent six months as a quadriplegic, at the mercy of diapers and caregivers, mind imprisoned in body. Guilherme will never forget the horror of impotence, the hospital nurse who threw a telephone at his paralyzed body. When his big toe moved his sheets, he concluded it was a miracle. God had granted him time to prepare for death. Then Guilherme chose the song of his final days.

Expelled from the World

Noêmia Atela came to not stay. She reiterates her commitment to resistance every day. She has reduced her life to the thirty steps that separate the door of her apartment from the bench at the end of the hall. There Noêmia sits, positioned between elevator and phone. Via one or the other, she expects her children to emancipate her. She is forever revealing the same secret: "Don't tell anyone. I'm leaving next week. I've asked my daughter to bring my suitcase."

"Out there" is how they've christened the world left behind— when in fact it is they who were left behind. A land where they have been, but will not be. Almost all came without a choice. First they lost their husband or wife, then it was their home they could no longer keep up, next their children's apartment got crowded, and finally the whole world transformed into a giant "Do Not Enter" sign. They were left with nowhere, with the home.

They arrived at the gate with the scraps of their dignity, their suitcases filled with their most cherished odds and ends, like pictures from their youth, from the time their kids were children and obeyed them, the days when the reins of life lay in their hands— hands that didn't fail them while gripping the balustrade. "It's just for a while, until you get better," their relatives said. And for the last time, they pretended to believe them.

"I came as a guest, to stay a few months. It wasn't even me who decided. I think they had a nice little talk and decided to give it a try. Then the stay got extended and now I expect to die here," says Maria Prado, a retired civil servant. With a century of mischief in her eye, she says: "I hope your stay doesn't get extended . . ."

For most residents of the home, the exit door is barred. They go out only with authorization. The ones who rule over their comings and goings are relatives or doctors. The residents might get lost, run over, or mugged. Beyond the gate, everything gets risky. Even for those with permission, the urge to see the city slowly wanes, eventually dying out. Until they cut the umbilical cord completely, and then the home becomes the world itself, its walls imbued with unrelenting security. "Sometimes I think about going out there. But what can I do out there, old like this?" asks Guilherme. "I only feel safe here, inside."

First time around, Paulo stayed only a month. A confirmed bachelor, he was living in his own apartment in Copacabana, assisted by caregivers after an accident immobilized his legs and a myocardial infarction ran over his heart. When his sister decided to spend a month in Europe, she asked Paulo to stay at the home. "Just so I don't worry," she said. Paulo went.

Then he returned to Copacabana. "That's when I realized. I was out walking with my cane and I saw a hulking shadow of a thing leap onto the counter at the café. It was a Doberman," he says. "When I was heading back to my place, some damn housewife was out gabbing with a friend, and next to her was the Doberman, without a leash. The next day it was a Doberman and a pit bull. I thought: 'If these tricksters come at me, what do I do?'"

Paulo called up a gun shop, ready to buy a pistol to defend himself. "Then I remembered my grandfather. He said I was too hot-headed to own a weapon. I'd end up doing something stupid," he says. "I gave away my pictures, blender, washing machine. I rented out my apartment and came back here. I had to accept my impotence. I no longer have the physical competence to go around out there."

If the world is dangerous for everyone, for the elderly it is a minefield. Every pothole in the sidewalk could be fatal, every extra stair step a promotion from cane to wheelchair. Their tired feet are no longer able to reach the bus where the driver is snorting his impatience over "these old folks who ride for free, and make us late to boot." When kids on the street make the elderly a prime target of robbery, in a clash between two groups of the vanquished, abandoned children and forsaken old people, the old people's legs don't obey the orders sent by adrenaline. This is how they are gradually expelled.

Their greatest fear is not of dying but of falling. "I've learned I'm on an island surrounded on all sides by the sea," Portuguese-born Fermelinda says. "I got here eighteen months ago and I'm afraid to go out. When I do, I feel like a bird on the wing. But I don't like flying anymore. If I fly, I might fall."

Those who can still walk on their own two feet, like Fermelinda, wander about the home as if they were in a medieval castle. They fear the second floor of the São Joaquim Pavilion more than Judgment Day. "Have you been there?" Fermelinda asks. "Better not go. If you insist, okay. But don't call me."

Those who fell and never got up again are on that floor. It is a place of long infirmaries where having dementia may be a better fate than being lucid, of human remains who let food fall from their mouths, who repeat movements from the past that make no sense now, and who call out for those who have gone. The second floor of São Joaquim rises up like a purgatory for living souls, a warehouse between home and cemetery. The residents pretend they are unaware of the latter—to the extent you can ignore the dark clouds that come before the storm.

Living Hours

Rosa Pimentel fell, from the third to the second floor of São Joaquim Pavilion, just one flight, the precipice. Rosa can only move her arms, but she has a mouth. And at eighty-eight, she isn't tired of reinventing life. Lying on one of the beds in the ward of those who have lost almost everything, including their minds, Rosa keeps afloat by versifying. Threading one line to another, she frees herself. "I don't know how it happens, because I never owned a poetry book," she says with a certain wonder. "The verses just come into my head."

No love, no money, not even any relatives, and now no movement either, Rosa has transformed her life into verse. "I was born on October eighteenth, in nineteen hundred thirteen, one fine

Saturday, at four twenty in the afternoon, Laranjeiras Street number 57, telephone number 357." She intersperses childhood with poetry: "I'm a nobody today, except to those who love me anyway. The biggest farm in Portugal belonged to my dad. I still recall the cows, Fancy, Ferreira, Fair Lady, and Beauty. And the white dog with the freckled speckles, Diamond was his name."

Rosa stretches out her arms, knowing she'll be alive as long as she continues to fit one verse into another. After all, isn't that how it is, a sad poem within a happy one, a loss within a gain, one day after the other?

Noêmia appears at her apartment door with a page from a notebook, crumpled from being clutched so hard. It has the days of the week on it, Monday through Sunday. Compass in hand, Noêmia navigates. "Is today Wednesday?" she asks. "Then it's the day my daughter Georgete visits. Saturdays it's my granddaughter who comes." She turns back into her room convinced she holds time in her hands.

Time is different at the home, governed by meals, the hands of the clock marking breakfast at seven thirty, a snack at ten, lunch at noon, another snack at two thirty, supper at five. If they live alone, they eat in their rooms; on the dormitory terraces if they share a space. There used to be a common dining room, but it quickly became apparent that the rich don't want to mix with the poor even in their old age. The payers were irritated by the poor manners of the nonpayers, by their haste, by the anxiousness of those who know the food might vanish from their plates.

They closed the dining hall, and meals are now served in the niches that fall to each class, so nobody's eyes will be offended by other people's hunger. The residents who aren't there as charity cases have decided to reprise the worst of the world they left behind. They've divided the home into North Side and South Side, and people from one don't mix with people from the other.

The elderly, not having much else to look forward to, look forward to their food. They structure their lives around the intervals between a little bread and butter and some fruit, between pizza and soup. So food acquires a disproportionate importance and becomes a topic at every ombudsman meeting. Disgusted with the orange root that doggedly occupies his life, Guilherme unleashes a crusade against carrots, eager for other colors, even if merely the washed-out hue of a potato. "I can't stand carrots anymore. It's carrots with stew, carrots with chicken, carrots in the salad. Why not potatoes?" he asks in public rebellion. "I'm turning orange." And he blushes instantly, gaining hints of beet.

Vicente Amorim longs for more refined dishes, presses for more sophisticated flavors, for spices that have departed. What he can't stand is having his menu defined, a poor metaphor for the free will he has lost. "The day I handed power of attorney over to my daughter, I signed away my own personality. First came a sense of elation. Then I woke up," he says. "I wouldn't have to worry about the bank anymore, knowing whether I was in the red or the black. That's when I lost my independence. But I didn't lose my mind."

This is the prison of the man who is always seated on the same bench at the home, protected by an angel's wings—a spot so entirely his that whenever he approaches in his wheelchair, whoever is usurping his space gets up immediately. "I never imagined I'd be here. Clinically, I'm not in any pain. But I feel an angst I can't explain, that I don't have any words to slip on my finger."

Vicente is a lonely one, so needy for company that he distances himself from everybody. Sweet Vicente, who at ninety-seven still harbors the illusion that he is sour. "I'm the stuck-up kind. I think I'm better than others, even knowing it's a stupid prejudice. And that's why I isolate myself," he confides. "So I started thinking this bench here is mine. I keep company with a little bird that flies down from the tree, with the sun that's crawling across the building. I observe the guy who's working, the one who's pretending to work, the one who makes easy money. I know the lives of everyone in this whole home. So I think I'm alone in the middle of a crowd. And I listen to the silence."

Sandra Carvalho has grown used to the silence. And to the days. "The girl comes in with my breakfast. Then I go downstairs. At eleven o'clock, I go back up to wait for lunch. Then I rest. Then I go downstairs. Then I go back up for supper. On Tuesdays and Thursdays, I do physical therapy for my knee. I keep on living," she says. Her children and grandchildren smile at her from their pictures on her dresser.

The Time of Lies

They told everyone they wanted to rest. "Telling lies is also a state of satisfaction," explains Vicente Amorim, seated beneath his stone angel's wings. Resting is precisely what he doesn't want to do. Who would, with eternity lurking just around the next corner?

The Portuguese word *asilo*, or asylum, became too cruel for an era that hides its brutality behind words. So they invented the expression "rest home" to give refuge to old people who were supposedly tired of life, when in fact the world was tired of them. "But this is really an asylum. A fancy one, but an asylum," Paulo flares up. "When I was younger, if someone had told me I'd be here, I'd say the guy was nuts. Golden years my ass!"

Rosa Bela gets up from the bench, wringing her hands like a character in a tragic drama, to say she doesn't want peace and quiet. "What's missing is that enthusiasm of young people who encourage old folks to cheer up. Instead of leaving the old folks just sitting and staring, like they're taking part in some old story. It's not some old story. It's real," she says. "Why can't we take part?" She sits back down, eyes shining, flooded with clarity.

Rosa rises from the bench once again, suddenly excited by the rare opportunity to be heard. Rosa, who always had so many ideas about everything, is sentenced to filling the empty hours at the home with the solitary echo of her words alone. She would like to share her tardy conclusion with the world. Now that she has finally discovered what was missing, there's no one to listen to her. "Here's the thing. An author writes well. The person who comes along later has already read what he wrote. So it's all similar. And that's how it's gone with everything. You don't get that feeling anymore of 'here's a new thing.' That's what's missing in the world. 'A new thing' to make it worth it," she says, interjecting phrases in English. Sitting a few feet away from Rosa is the young girl who watches over the floor during endless nights filled with insomnia and moans. She thinks Rosa is crazy.

The Time of Truths

Peopled by more than twenty thousand years of life, sum total, the home inhales, exhales, seems to move. Since its foundation, management has been handed down from heir to heir, pursuant to a clause in a will. It has now reached Regina Bittencourt, nearly eighty, a *grande dame* and ambassador's wife, the kind who was suckled on French and weaned on forays around the world. Dona Regina is heir to two dying breeds of institutions: aristocracy and charity. She modernized the home by opening its doors to paying clients, because donations had dried up when large fortunes did. The family tradition is being carried on, her daughter and grandson slated to ensure continuity.

The place is surrounded on all sides by saints and noblemen. Every fountain or garden bed has a name, and a very long one. It is a strange setting in which to learn that one of the few advantages of old age is the removal of a human relations tumor: hypocrisy. Even when they're ambushed by the traps of a tired brain, the residents display razor-sharp objectivity. "I don't like to be called elderly. I'm just plain old!" says centenarian Maria Prado, whose mouth has dispensed with both teeth and cynicism. "Have you ever seen a pretty old lady? She might be sad, resigned, happy. Happy—I don't think there is a one. Some are resigned, others less so. But pretty, not a one."

They have reached an age where all pretenses are as expendable as an appendix. Maybe that is why it is so convenient that they stay locked up inside. At the end of every month, the home has a party to celebrate all the birthdays. The event is sponsored by socialites from Rio de Janeiro on charity missions. Some years back, the home would bring in celebrities to put on shows, but they eventually stopped. One of the victims was Pelé. Social climber Kiki Garavaglia dies laughing when she tells how the King sang a "little ditty for the old folks." Indifferent to his majesty, one of the elderly women shouted out: "Sing something else. Boy, that's just awful!" Pelé discovered at the home that he has the voice of Edson Arantes do Nascimento.

These monthly parties result in priceless scenes. Socialite Gisela Amaral always arrives late. If she arrives. So when the residents learn that Gisela drew their name and has been assigned to give them a gift, they are immediately depressed. At the age of sixty-one, with the figure of a forty-one-year-old, Gisela bursts in dressed top to bottom in mustard yellow, Bombom and Banana in tow. Bombom is her driver and Banana, her dog. Announcement over the microphone: "Gisela Amaral, just in from New York. Look how Gisela's darling shoes match her outfit!" Gisela shows off her shoes. The old folks are agape. They have lived for this.

The Swordplay of the Sexes

Noêmia has lived eighty-six years to confirm yet another dubious victory for women: old age is female. "What we don't have here are men," she says. "When one shows up, it's a joy." There are three women for every man at the home. While women may live longer, they seem sentenced to loneliness, an equation that grows more lopsided each year, according to the list of residents.

More than statistics, what hampers autumn love is the same thing that used to foil romance in sunnier seasons. The women soon realize that men, even in their old age, continue to take everything very seriously, especially themselves. Were it not for this atavistic facet of the male personality, a verdant spring would probably blossom forth in this cranny of the world. "Dating is ridiculous at our age," declares Guilherme. "I don't like jowls," sneers Paulo. "Or fossils."

Given his impossible aspiration, Paulo prefers to consummate his sexual fantasies cradled by photos and a video of Cyd Charisse, Fred Astaire's "beautiful dynamite," as she was known in Brazil. Her status of unattainable muse protects him forever from any awareness of the inevitable actuality of her "jowls." Cyd Charisse, in flesh and blood, is almost eighty years old, and her coveted legs likely exhibit a road map of varicose veins. Paulo's Cyd is still twenty, thirty, absolute master that he is of his object of desire.

Although their feet don't move as steadily, the women keep them planted on the floor, as practical in old age as in their youth. They sigh over soap opera stars but never forget to look around them in search of what is possible. "I'm in love. I think he gets nervous when he sees me," Fermelinda says, melting. "My dream is that we'll share a suite here at the home someday." Fermelinda straightens and messes up her bed several times a day, when all she would really like to do is the same thing, but in fine company.

While the man she loves remains as distant as the Christ statue atop Corcovado, Fermelinda's Rio de Janeiro is always at 100 degrees Fahrenheit. "There's no such thing as a frigid woman or a cold one. You know what a cold woman is? Someone who doesn't have the brains for love," she says. "Men never die. You just need a woman who knows how to get him ready." At this point, Fermelinda is waving a very big fan.

The thermometer at the home spiked dangerously high four months ago when Robert Regard, a Frenchman, appeared at the gate sporting a still-respectable assemblage of muscles. At the age of sixty-two—just a kid by local standards, which average around eighty-five—he found himself homeless following a twenty-four-year romance with a Brazilian hairdresser.

Robert was a bit leery as he crossed the portico, but soon discovered there was no better balm for his scuffed self-esteem. He planted himself in the patio wearing shorts and a tank top. At each throb of his biceps, a female heart did a triple somersault. To top it off, the pecs all came with an accent. "Women love it when I speak French," he says.

The Alain Delon of the home was crowned Mister France in 1967 and made a career in European weightlifting. At the age of thirty-seven, he left his wife and five children and ventured down to Brazil, where he opened two supermarkets, went bankrupt, managed several other grocery stores, and ended up with nothing, except for a Brazilian daughter and an unconditional love for his adopted homeland. He puffs up with pride over the hubbub he incites, but he doesn't even consider the possibility of getting involved with one of the women who share his exile. "They're my friends. I don't lead anyone on," he explains. "I've always had younger girls running after me. I see myself with a forty- or forty-five-year-old. That's why I keep my weight at 180, don't eat supper, get my exercise. I'm in good shape."

Women are always more pragmatic. It's no wonder they live longer. Without any partners to dance with at the home, they waltz across the floor with their girlfriends, the nurses, the caregivers. Theirs was a generation when a woman's world was confined to the home, and this latest phase out of an entire existence has taught them to live between walls. In a way, they have lost a little less and a little more, as they can't suffer over what they never knew.

Not the men. Their world was out there, masters of all beyond, control over every step. Now they posture themselves as grumps, afraid of "being an embarrassment," refusing to do battle with the legs they have. They don't tolerate the limitations of old age as well, dependent on much younger girls who are there not because the men are so seductive, but to change their diapers. More ravaged by the winds of melancholy, the men languish while the women play the accordion, the piano, or write verses.

"I've fallen down, played music, sung songs, gotten back up, cried, let it go. And now I'm here. I wake up with all that music," says lyric singer Mariluza Prista. "There's no advantage whatsoever to reaching this wretched age, when you depend on others even to take a shower," shoots Fernando Ferreira, a former dentist. "I can't even smoke or drink anymore. I'm waiting for death. Everyone should only live to fifty."

Out on the balcony, Noêmia has decided to hear only what she wants. "Good thing I'm deaf," she says. Suddenly she lights up. Explicit sex scenes are unfolding nearby, accompanied by scandalous wailing. This time Noêmia hears quite well. Being considerate, she knocks on her neighbor's door: "Come quick! Let's watch the cats mating on the roof."

Possible Loves

Only cat love makes noise at the home. Old people's love is bashful. They carry their shame in with them, and inside, it hardens into cement. Adyr Galvão Bueno and Gabriela Svozil have been weaving a romance of whispers for years, afraid of offending the small world where they live off charity. The couple tries to make themselves invisible to avoid glaring looks from those who think the chance for love ends when the first wrinkle is born. They repeat their scenes, side by side on the bench, almost apologetic, lacking courage to hold hands, killing the kiss before it happens. Even so, somebody always points a finger, stiffened not by age but by pettiness: "Ridiculous."

Only the couple themselves see beauty in the dramatic way they met—her, fallen across the breakfast table, sick to her stomach; him, so thin that there is little difference between side and front views, carrying her in his scrawny arms to one of the beds in the ward for the poor. Since then, they're always seen together, always shy. Her, the widow of a man who said little. Him, still waiting for the fiancée who traveled to Belgium decades ago and never returned. They don't flee the home on outings because Gabriela can only handle escapes of a few steps. Nor does Adyr give her flowers, because you aren't allowed to pick them from the gardens.

They'll never share a bed, because they can't afford a private suite. When night falls and the entire population of old folks town takes refuge within the safety of walls, Adyr and Gabriela experience the most intimate moments of their romance. They go to sleep aflame, fearful of being expelled, like boarding school children experimenting with prohibited games at recess. From the veranda of the men's dormitory, Adyr waves a towel so that Gabriela's weary eyes can divine him at their latest farewell.

In another bed in the building, Manoel Matias is thinking about Maria Socorro. They filled out the registration form at the home years ago, recording plainly: "For the first time, we're going to sleep apart." They made a point to add: "We will always be together in our vision of a happy life." The couple exchanged goodbyes from the doors of their respective dormitories, after sleeping in each other's arms for sixty years. In the rickety bed they left behind, they had shared the pain of children that didn't come, of the family business that never became a reality, of Maria's hands wearing out from the pots and pans at her boss's house, of Manoel's miseries behind a shop counter owned by someone else.

Every morning, Manoel and Maria reunited again. He was eighty-six, she was ninety-four. They spent their days holding fast to each other to make up for the emptiness of every night. Suddenly she fell ill, and wasn't seen in the garden anymore. Then Manoel would get up, well-groomed and cologned, and go visit his Maria. Ever more silent, she started drifting out of Manoel's reach. Still, he didn't give up on touching her. "I don't complain. We never had anything of our own, but we went through life without fighting. It was love at first sight," he says. "And I always let her decide everything."

Manoel continues to visit his Maria, who in May decided it was time to depart. "She's quieter and quieter, doesn't say hardly a thing," Manoel says uncomplainingly. He's a realist about everything else, but not about Maria's death. He takes a shower for her and combs tapioca powder through his hair for her. To him, Maria is always as lovely as that day in Copacabana when he first set eyes on her, his heart leaping from his chest and never more belonging to him. Whenever Manoel sits in the library, he saves a spot beside him. It's for Maria. Maybe, Manoel ventures, she'll cheer up and come.

Joaquim Cysneiros Vianna goes to give Aurea a kiss every day. And every day Aurea finds that Joaquim left long ago. Attorneys, both of them. Joaquim, brilliant; Aurea, independent at a time when women were just beginning to taste freedom. Their life was built of protest rallies, trips to Europe, an everyday routine of books and long conversations. Seven years ago, Joaquim began slipping away. The man with whom Aurea had shared her life had been kidnapped by Alzheimer's disease. The courtroom star was soon a boy, no table manners, fleeing from his bath, running away from home.

"Fight back," Aurea got tired of screaming. He couldn't hear her anymore. Joaquim arrived at the home first, brought by their daughter. Aurea came one year ago, her legs robotized by arthrosis.

She refused to stay in the same apartment as her husband. "He's not here anymore, he's trapped inside himself. He's not living, he's vegetating. He's become something else and it's very hard to see him like this," she says. "All he does is kiss me and say 'yeah,' the only word that's left."

Now another woman takes care of Joaquim, the caregiver Maria José Ferreira, who at the age of forty-six already fears her own old age. She puts lotion on Joaquim's skin less for the pay and more out of affection. She makes sure his clothes match, makes sure he joins in the busy routine of activities at the home, even if only with his body, so he doesn't leave for good. His daughter Angela calls every day, always at one o'clock, to force her dad to talk. Even if only to hear a sequence of "yeahs."

Angela is a rarity at a place where visitors are more absent than its residents would like. The single mother of an adult son, Angela the educator shows up at the gate twice a week and with every appearance delights the entire floor with tasty treats from her kitchen. When her father and mother started to fail, they moved in with her. The challenges were so many and so awful that she had to quit her job at the university. "It gave me a horrendous guilt complex when I had to bring my dad here. I only understood later that there was no getting around it," she says. "Then my mom came. There was no way we could share the same space anymore either. She's always been independent and authoritarian. She had lost her home, her husband, and her life, and she was driving me crazy. Her doctor said if I didn't make a decision, I'd be the one to expire."

Aurea survives by relinquishing the verb *want*. "I'd like to stay with my daughter, but there's a big distance between the will and the way," she says. "To avoid disappointment, I try not to want anything. I've learned that here. I've accepted it. A person who lives learns by living."

What remains for Aurea is lucidity. Not always a blessing.

Class Struggle

For the wealthy, old age may be more painful because it is made up only of losses. Everything slips through the hands of the elderly, especially power and choice, from diet to living place. They are powerless to choose with whom they share quandaries and companionship, and humiliated by their dependence on strangers, even to take a bath. The poor arrive at the gate carrying a suitcase containing less clothing and a greater ability to reinvent themselves. Forever reduced to the minimum, they come skilled in the art of seizing possibilities. Their lamentations have always died in their chest.

Rossi Rodrigues, retired seamstress, discovered if she accepted the world of the living, she would end up departing for the world of the dead, a misfortune that always seemed in very bad taste to her. "Lord help me!" she exclaims with a grimace. Rossi came here seventeen years ago because she is not someone to live with a son or shove herself into her daughter-in-law's corner. She uses the home like a hotel. Since she doesn't have to worry about what tormented her throughout her youth—food and housing—there's more time to poke around where she shouldn't.

As a composer of Brazilian *brega* music, what Rossi really enjoys is mending the world. In her old age, she is making the dream of her youth come true, earning respect both inside the home and out. She is well informed enough to remind the rich, during the surliness of their inevitable clashes, that if it weren't for the poor, the home would lose out on philanthropic contributions and no longer be tax exempt.

Early each morning, Rossi listens to a series of radio programs to set her schedule. There's not a single protest where her flag isn't hoisted high, no accusation that she doesn't investigate with her own eyes, no debate in which she doesn't voice her opinion, no lecture at which she doesn't learn at least a new word. She is involved in the Catholic Church's health care ministry, prison ministry, and as many others as she can. Rossi was there at Candelária, protesting the mass murder of street children; at Santa Genoveva Clinic, protesting the abuse, neglect, and deaths of the elderly; and at the World Social Forum, protesting capitalism's murderous savagery. She has been to Brasilia more than once.

She never tires of dismaying the home with her T-shirt collection, the most eye-catching of which bears the initials of the Landless Workers Movement. "I came here to live, not die," she proclaims. Rossi looks in the mirror, checks her wrinkles, and touches them one by one to make sure they're all in the right place. "I love these wrinkles of mine. Each one a son, a grandchild, my life."

Anyone who sees this devotee of Saint Hedwig at mass, knees scraping on the ground, cannot even begin to suspect what is going on inside that head of salt-and-pepper hair, in that sweet heart beating so earnestly inside a flowered granny dress. "Look, I'll tell you," and she does: "If I weren't so Catholic, I'd bomb the president's office in Brasilia."

Gentle as a peppercorn, she stirs up her "comrades." "Let's get out of here," she shouts. "Ah, Rossi, I've got my life programmed out. A dormitory to sleep in, cafeteria to eat in, chapel to pray in, infirmary for when I get sick. And then the cemetery in Caju." Good lord! Rossi can't stand it. Out she goes again, wielding her purse, always late for the world outside. "If I was some cute girl, then you'd pull over!" she curses the bus driver who ignores her at the stop. "Don't you have a mother, young man? You're not going to get old?" She whips out her notebook to take down his license number.

She leaves her roommates, Santinha and Sebastiana, saying their rosaries. At ninety-two, Santinha couldn't care less. She was Dulcelina Maria Corrêa seventy-eight years ago when she came to the home to starch shirts. She was fourteen and still playing hopscotch. Santinha ended up spending her life here, inside these walls, in the very illustrious company of the viscount, in his various bronze poses.

She fell in love with Joel the carpenter when he was adding some new wings to the home and got married in the chapel lined with Belgium tiles under the eyes of Louis IX, or Saint Louis, the so-called holy king of France. She lost her virginity and two of her three children under that decrepit roof; took her third child, Maria Luiza, to the altar; prayed over her husband's casket; and, last of all, grew old.

They only realized what had happened in 1957. Then Santinha the staff member was promoted to resident and, because she accepts everything, was cloaked in sainthood in life. "I can't believe I've grown old here," she says in amazement, while feeding a legion of stray cats and lice-infested pigeons. Nothing else amazes her.

Not Noêmia. She was amazed—and utterly so—that her seven children lodged her in the home after they had concluded she'd become impossible. They had held a meeting in which they even kept minutes. "Your mother was almost run over," a neighbor had called to say. "She's trying to buy cigarettes again," the baker had warned, aware of Noêmia's emphysema, brought on by three packs a day.

She had gone so far as to concoct scenes of horror to earn visits and attention, like the day she called near death to report that the maid had attacked her. There was Noêmia, stretched across the floor, her bosom bloodied with tomato sauce. Once, the tranquilizer the doctor had prescribed for Noêmia was taken by one of her daughters when the charming tyrant went to spend a shortened stay at her home.

"I can't abide staying here, staring at nothing," Noêmia grumbles. Soon she convinces a kind soul to take her to the phone. List in hand, she calls each of her seven children plus some grandchildren to remind them for the umpteenth time that her bags are packed.

Stolen Youth

The home that is death for Noêmia is, for another breed of women, not only life but the most generous portion of their puny slice of existence. Every day that was stolen from their youth, they dreamed of the home. They yearned for the moment when their arms could no longer wash, iron, cook, or scrub, when nothing but the walls of the home would be left to contain their sighs of exhaustion. These women are part of a dynasty where life was sad. Where old age is a blessing because even if people wanted to exploit them, they couldn't anymore. Sucked dry of everything, there is nothing more to rip from their bodies, and so they are emancipated to die.

Laurentina Francisca de Jesus sprang from these roots. She's a wisp of a woman, her skin worn by drought, like Bahia's arid *sertão* region, from which she hails. "My plan was something gentle God gave me. It was traced out here, in this home, the place where I'd be happy," she says, beginning her narrative in the poetic prose that seems to germinate in the very placentas of people from the Northeast, as if the gentleness of their souls might offset the harshness of the land.

"I was birthed in Amargosa, a town that once was Nossa Senhora do Bom Conselho and then they changed its name, I never knew what for. No father, no mother, I worked in the fields like a man. One day they took me off to Rio de Janeiro and I went on working without earning a penny. From there I went to another house, and they didn't pay me either. I even had bad thoughts about killing myself, but then I prayed: 'Our Lady of mine, with the child that is in your arms, help me. Give me a rest home, in life or in death.' Then God gave me this home. And I've been happy ever since."

That's Laurentina, plain and simple. Hasn't missed a thing since she freed herself from her cage and became a bird. Not one outing, or party, or any program at the home takes place without Laurentina taking her place at it. She discovered everything once she was old, from peace and quiet to sand on the beach. At the age of eighty-four, the only reason she hasn't been up Sugarloaf is that, upon arriving there, she lacked the courage to jump into the cable car. Having already achieved so much, she thought leaping hills was far too daring.

They took nearly everything from her, even her hair, her only adornment, chopped off by a woman she worked for in order to make a wig. Laurentina never voted a single time in her life, since she remained unfamiliar with her ABCs and nobody did her the favor of telling her she could sign with her finger. She never knew the pain or the sweetness of a man, because her reply to the three good-for-nothings who happened her way was the same: "Not interested, not even with sugar." What remained for Laurentina was this resignation mingled with a wisdom that keeps those of her lot alive.

Women like Laurentina nestle the first toys of their lives upon their rest beds. There is irony in these dolls, so tardy they missed childhood and arrived only at the end of life, simulacra of the children the women didn't have because they were too busy raising other people's. "I raised my boss's kids and grandkids. When I got there, their boy was real little. When I left, he was married. I miss him. Wish he'd visit me," says Amália Bernardina Gomes. "Every little penny I made, I gave my boss to put in savings. When there was some fat profit in there, he put me in a car and left me here. My dream was to come to the rest home. I haven't got anyone, not even visitors. My only family is God."

Amália, also from the Northeast, spends her days looking after Denise, the washed-out doll someone gave her. "Hi, honey, Mommy's here!" she greets her, all devotion and selflessness, a woman born deaf and mute to the idea of complaining. "Thank God I've got nothing to say. My life's been real good. I was born to die."

Less resigned is Maria de Lourdes Silva, whose name nobody knows because everyone calls her Lourdinha Lavadeira, Lourdes the Washer Woman. She was born beating clothes clean on a stone, the soap that seeped into her skin the only perfume in her life. At the age of four, she was taken from her mother to keep the company of a fine lady's daughter. Then she followed this fortune, raising José Augusto and José Flávio in Minas, Ana and Alexandre in Rio de Janeiro. When Lourdinha fell sick one day, the home was what remained for her.

Without any choice then as now, Lourdinha stayed right where she was. At the age of sixty-two, she found a way to earn some spare change by washing the clothes that the richer women prefer to see beaten by her hands, their lifelines somewhat faded by the rivers of water that erode into her palms day after day. "I do my washing, make a little money to buy some fruit, some sweets and such, any little out-of-the-ordinary something I get an urge to eat."

Always alone because she is, in her own words, a real perfectionist, Lourdinha gets upset when her roommates hang clothes on the beds, fight with each other, or exit the bathroom with dripping underwear in their hands. Lourdinha no less, who has always liked everything just so, ended up living amid the disorder of a crowd. "You know, I've got this way: I stretch the clothes good, shake out the sleeves, slide them between my fingers to smooth them." She says this with pride, gesturing the story, holding herself high, mistress at least of the impeccable creases on her shirts, the pleats on every blouse, at the only moment when she holds her fate in her hands. Even if nobody else notices, Lourdinha is certain that no clothing in this world is as well washed as hers. And that seems enough for her.

Chiquinha, her plastic daughter and only company, waits for her in the baby carriage. "She even laughs for me," Lourdinha says dotingly. "She takes after me, this little girl of mine."

The Day After

The home slides into nighttime before the world does. At five o'clock, the serving of soup announces curfew. Silence descends indifferent to the sun still illuminating the rooftops, to the far-off rumble from the streets. The iron gate swings shut. With shuffling footsteps, the residents retreat to their rooms to weave their coverlets of loneliness. Lying in their beds, they pretend to sleep so the little time they have left passes even more quickly. They brave the insomnia broken by the frights that form old age.

In the darkness, sitting in a rocking chair, few know it but Lourdinha is waiting. She has assigned herself the task of turning on the lights in the gardens. At five in the morning, she'll be in the same place, this time to turn them off. Her silhouette cuts in and out between statues of saints and viscounts in her task of tying one cycle to another. She's the one who ensures the continuity of life at the old people's home.

"Don't be frightened," Noêmia says reassuringly. "The nurses come into our rooms all the time at night. But it's just to make sure we're okay." She shuts the door to her room, complains yet again about no longer having the key to either her door or her life, and in mistrustful silence checks to see that her fortune is still tucked safely beneath her mattress. Only then can Noêmia sleep. She doesn't realize the bills are pretend, borrowed from a grandson's board game.

Protected in their rooms, the residents fool everyone. They resist. Lying in his bed, his cane leaning against an armchair, Paulo laughs so hard he cries. His laughter smothers the pain of a neighbor lady who chains the hours together with interludes of moaning. He reminisces about all the trouble he got into in his youth. Then, awash in tears, he sews one dream to another. He usually holds tight to oneiric wings as he flies. If he's lucky, he has "erotic

dreams about Dr. Gisele, Dr. Ana Lúcia, Soraia my physical thera-
pist . . ." If he's especially inspired, he kicks Fred Astaire off the
stage with a spin, betrays all the women in his life, and dances cheek
to cheek with Cyd Charisse.

Maria Prado can sleep only with the help of pills. Every day she
prepares to wake up in another world, wholly at peace. "At the age
of 101, I've reached the conclusion that I've got nothing to boast
about, nothing to be ashamed of." Nothing. She opens her eyes
and there she is, between the same walls, newspaper at her door.
"Where has this bin Laden gotten to?" she inquires, nothing more
interesting to do. "At least let me end before the world does!"

In another wing, Vicente Amorim only shuts his eyes once he
has checked the stock market. "I'm not in charge of my money
anymore, but I can't sleep without waiting for the latest stock report," he says, surprised at himself. Then he has nightmares. "I'm
swimming in a river and can't reach the bank. I try to grab hold
of something, but I can't. Then I wake up. For a few seconds, it all
seems real. I have to breathe deep, look hard at the walls. Then I
think: Well, I'm alive. At that moment, it's good to be alive."

Guilherme is grateful to life only because it gives him time to
repent of all his sins. He laments the flesh that tempted him so
much and to which he always succumbed. "Flesh, flesh. Today's
pleasures, worthless tomorrow. I only hope God takes me gently."
While Guilherme is lashing his soul, Fermelinda tosses and turns
for the opposite reason. Despairing because she cannot sin, she cov-
ers herself with rashes. For want of caresses, her body is wrapped in
allergies.

Rosa Bela keeps watch from the hall. Across the way, shackled
to her bed, an elderly woman mixes flat notes with moans. "You
notice what she does?" Rosa asks in distress. "She makes her own
melody. Sings herself a lullaby. I hear it from my room and it nearly
drives me crazy." Rosa gets up, stretches her arms into the void of

the deserted hallway. Her eyes burn as she sings, her voice scorching like fire. She stifles the other woman's pain with the sound of an old love. Then she sinks into her room to rise with the sun. "Here is a new day for you, and you take it and like it!" she says in English. And suddenly Rosa is moving the furniture around.

Noêmia turns her back to the home and embarks on her return journey. For now she has won; a daughter has rescued her. She steps through the iron gate, her whole life squeezed into a carry-on.

THE COLLECTOR OF LEFTOVER SOULS

Bagé, in Porto Alegre, would be a street like any other in the neighborhood of Petrópolis. It would be, were it not for house number 81. A sliver of chaos in the cosmic order of Bagé. A triangle in the middle of a row of squares. A raw protest against consumer society, disposable and implacable. Number 81 Bagé Street is the lair of a little man, not even five feet tall, frail as a sigh: Oscar Kulemkamp. Inside the house lie fragments of an entire city.

Nobody knows when Oscar Kulemkamp initiated his resistance. He spends day after day on a pilgrimage through the streets of Porto Alegre. He began by rescuing amputated stools and giving them back their legs. Eventually he took on the mission of gathering up bits and pieces of the city. He goes from trash bin to trash bin, as far as he can, retrieving chunks of wood and pipe, broken fans, cracked vases, abandoned toys. It is an arduous task, because he's a lone combatant against an army of 1.3 million people who toss out the remnants of their lives every day.

Oscar Kulemkamp has reclaimed these cast-off lives and saved them from the landfill of oblivion. That's how the simple house where he raised seven children was transformed into a lair. Remnants of existence have gradually taken over the rooms of his home. When the inside overflowed, he began occupying the front yard, the breezeway, the backyard. When every space was filled, he began hanging things from the branches of the chinaberry and avocado trees. After the trees, it was the sidewalk's turn. Oscar Kulemkamp's cocoon would not stop growing. Now the windows are covered by obsolescent things, and he can only penetrate the house by snaking through a tunnel of remains.

If he weren't reinventing the world, Oscar Kulemkamp would merely be the owner of a life that had departed. Like his wife did, four years ago. And a daughter, lost to cancer. For most of his eighty-five years he was a waiter, but the tables he served no longer exist. They are names from the past, thin air, like Sherazade Restaurant. Stories no longer told, streets now gone, characters that inhabit only cemeteries.

He emerges from his timeless tunnel like a little mole. He is wearing cheap clothing, threadbare and dingy from the dust of days. He's deafer than a doornail, as he puts it. If he didn't salvage the remains of other people's existences, he'd only have the two sons who share his cave, one who lives in darkness and never leaves home, one who sometimes threatens to kill him. And the four married children who don't understand his obsession. And the two cats who wage never-ending battles with the squadron of rats who stalk this elderly inhabitant of Bagé.

Oscar Kulemkamp has stitched his patchwork from other people's lives, from the rubbish of other people's lives. Cards never sent to him: "I prayed so hard to spend this Christmas with you." Manuals for objects that never belonged to him: "Please note: this television set offers a number of innovative features. To understand and enjoy them all, it is essential that you begin by reading the instruction manual." Packages he never ordered: "Services paid for by check will only be delivered after the check has cleared." Strangers' IDs, business cards from professions never to be his. Magazine pages, leaflets, prayer cards. A photograph of a royal family, a picture of snow. Even a piece of paper that reads "I'm happy!" Christmas bulbs from a tree that didn't glow in his December.

In Oscar Kulemkamp's hideout, deflated balloons from the birthday party of a child he doesn't know adorn every day of his life. A decoration some other child made from Popsicle sticks—later abandoned by the mother who received it—is housed in the living room cupboard. Twisted, broken, beat-up dolls sit in a row. And rejected little girls in smiling photos hang there like beloved granddaughters.

The neighbors are alarmed by the relentlessly expanding cocoon, by the shadows—half tree, half garbage—that advance into the street. One woman living nearby asked the Department of Urban Sanitation to do something about it, and they carried off part of Oscar Kulemkamp's treasure. He was driven to such despair that no one else has had the courage to protest. A sympathetic neighbor now keeps a hose at hand, so the day it all goes up in flames, he can at least save the man entrenched in his cave. Then Oscar Kulemkamp can resume his endless journey to save the bits and pieces of the city.

When he appears from within today, skeptical and smiling, Oscar Kulemkamp hurries to explain that one day, one day soon, he's going to carry it all off to build a beach house. A paradise where weary dolls, photos of children no longer loved, and cards from birthdays past do not turn into trash. A world where neither things nor people are disposable. Where nothing and nobody becomes obsolete once it is old, broken, or bent. A world where everyone is of equal value, and no one's lot is a garbage bin.

Number 81 Bagé Street is the castle of a man who has invented a world without leftovers. By assigning value to things that have none, Oscar Kulemkamp values himself. By collecting cast-off lives, Oscar Kulemkamp salvages his own. Perhaps this is the mystery of house number 81. And perhaps this is why it is so frightening.

LIVING MOTHERS OF A DEAD GENERATION

"When my third child died, I thought I'd die too, and so I bought a white polyester shroud. But it was my daughter who died. I wrapped her in the shroud meant for me."

Selvina Francisca da Silva lost four children; a fifth vanished.

She survived.

"It was unbearable knowing my son would end up killed. So I decided to set fire to us both."

Nobody sold alcohol to Maria Fátima da Silva Souza that day. As she feared, her son was murdered years later.

She survived.

"When my son showed up at home alive, but with a bullet in the chest, I started paying down on a casket. Now I'm making payments on my second son's. He's still alive, but I know he's going to die."

Enilda Rodrigues da Silva's oldest son was murdered just before Christmas.

She survived.

"My son took a bullet in the belly. It went straight through him. The police said the only trouble the family would have was burying him."

Josefa Inacio Farias's son was executed, stuffed into a plastic bag, and pitched down the stairs.

She survived.

"My third son was killed by a bullet in the chest at a drug den. He was twenty-two. I'd already lost my other two. My head pounds. It feels like there's a drum inside. I hear the sound day and night."

Eva Sebastiana Araújo lost three children.

She survived.

"I didn't go to the funeral of a single one of my children. If I could, I'd bury myself."

Three of Graça Mary Azevedo Carneiro's children were killed.

She survived.

"The first one that died was just a little thing, no bigger than this. Stabbed seventy-eight times. He was thirteen."

Helena Silva Cruz lost two sons. The third turned killer to avenge his brothers.

She survived.

"My son yelled out because he was losing a lot of blood. The police heard him, broke down the door, and he died. The traffickers paid for the burial."

Francisca Maria da Silva Porfirio's son lasted a year in the drug trade before he was killed.

She survived.

Gunfire has erased a generation of Brazilians from the future. Scenes of this extermination were portrayed in the documentary *Falcão*, by Brazilian rapper MV Bill and producer Celso Athayde, founder of the Central Union of Favelas (CUFA). The film shocked the country not for its news value, but for its brutality. Of the seventeen youth depicted in the movie, only one is still alive. *Falcão* showed that in the favelas of Brazil, the life expectancy for boys in drug trafficking is twenty. They're killed before they reach adulthood. Selvina, Maria, Enilda, Josefa, Eva, Graça, Helena, and Francisca are the Pietàs of the urban periphery. The living mothers of a dead generation.

A UNESCO study led by sociologist Julio Jacobo Waiselfisz found that guns are the leading cause of death among Brazilian youth. In the twenty-four years from 1979 to 2003, the country's population grew 52 percent while firearm homicides rose 543 percent—an increase attributable to teen murders. Of the 550,000 killed, almost half were between the ages of fifteen and twenty-four.

In these pages, the Brazilian drug war is revealed through the eyes and voices of mothers whose children died in its battles. These women's wombs bear foot soldiers (never generals) for the drug nation. Their children are felled by guns, knives, and grenades, not as special exceptions but as everyday events. When the women finish burying one child and turn around to find another in line, it pushes them one step beyond madness.

These deaths not only have an age; they also have a skin color and a social class. In a study on race and homicide victims in Brazil ("Cor e vitimização por homicídios no Brasil"), Rio de Janeiro State University researchers Ignacio Cano, Doriam Borges, and Eduardo Ribeiro established that the probability of being murdered is almost twice as high for Brazilians of mixed ethnicity and nearly three times as high for black people. Murder rates are higher where income is lower and public services more inadequate.

Drug trafficking ranks among the world's three most lucrative businesses. The mothers don't see any of this money, nor did their children, most of whom started wielding a gun before they'd finished primary school. They didn't even have time to learn where Colombia is. Trapped in the favela by the threat of the police and rival drug gangs, they spend their lives in the filthy back alleys of the only world they'll ever know, cornered and waiting for the next gunshot. In the words of historian Marcelo Freixo, researcher with the human rights organization Global Justice, these are "needy kids shooting at poor children."

This is the story of their mothers.

The Mutilated Mother

No language has a word for someone who outlives a child. This is a pain that defies verbal expression. Selvina, seventy-four, takes her breaths in a windowless room that sleeps seven. The air triggers coughing and waves of nausea. It would be impossible to breathe were Selvina's lungs not adapted to the impossible. Over the course of this life to which she clings so tightly, Selvina first lost her nails and then her fingers and toes—to burns, other accidents, disease. Stumps are all she has left, and with them she resists. Selvina stares at her mutilated limbs and says, "I wish life hadn't crippled me. I'm used up. Everything's gone."

There is no hyperbole in the prose of these living mothers. Their words are exact, their sentences lean. Selvina gave birth to twelve children. Four were shot to death. She's not sure about a fifth, who vanished. Another five died from sickness. Two remain. In this arithmetic of losses, she doesn't miss the ones who succumbed to the measles or the "evil eye." The pain that devastates her was left by the ones who were "murdered to death." This, says Selvina, is death that cannot be forgotten.

"I got to Brasilia on July 25, 1959, when Juscelino Kubitschek was president. I came from Piauí, where I went from one prospecting site to another. I sold a diamond in Copacabana, in Rio de

Janeiro, and went to Brasilia to get ahead in life. My name's Selvina Francisca da Silva."

Selvina arrived in Brasilia before the new federal capital had been inaugurated, but she never found a place there. Her sole contact with Oscar Niemeyer's architecture was as a housemaid, and she set foot in the heart of the planned city only to serve. She moved from squatter town to squatter town until planting her partial feet in the satellite city of Ceilândia, where she's a faith healer for the infirm. In exchange, her clients don't let her starve to death. She managed to bury three of her four murdered children "in the cemetery right inside Brasilia, the same place that Juscelino's buried." She had to bury the last one in Ceilândia instead, fighting over the price because she couldn't afford it. "I'm a Brazilian and I'm going to bury my daughter inside Brazil even if I have to dig her grave outside the cemetery," she told the man in charge.

Selvina is interrupted by her oldest granddaughter, orphan of the daughter who was killed in a shootout between drug traffickers. She's seventeen and pregnant. "Grandma, my water broke. I need to go to the hospital. I'm bleeding."

The girl clutches her big belly and lets out a moan. The baby's father is serving time for armed robbery. There was nothing to eat that morning. Selvina reacts with toughness to her granddaughter's despair. "Calm down there, girl. I don't have any money. You'll have to wait." She raises her mutilated hands to the sky: "My commander tells me to fear no one."

Knifed in the Womb

Eva woke up with her husband stabbing away at her. He shoved his knife up her vagina, trying to hit her uterus. "You're a snake that puts kids in the world to kill them," he shouted. Eva shows where the painful geography of her life has been mapped out across her body. Cigarette burns, stab wounds, the marks of beatings.

Another two sons were killed, and her husband believed more firmly in the original sin of his own Eve. "Now that the last one's dead, I want to see who's going to defend you," he said. When she was pregnant with their first, he kicked her in the belly, beat her with a steel rod, slashed her leg. He stomped on her foot until the skin split open. At thirteen, the son walked around with two guns tucked in his waistband. "Dad, I love you a whole lot, but if you touch Mom again, I'll kill you." And his father didn't. "Sometimes I think that's why they died. So they wouldn't kill their dad and miss out on God's salvation," says Eva of Brasilândia, a community on the northern periphery of São Paulo. "But he was a good father. He didn't beat them. Just me."

A drum pounds in Eva's head night and day. "I look up into heaven every day and can't believe I'm here and not in an insane asylum. I can't, I can't, I can't," she says. Eva repeats snippets of her sentences at least three times, as if she has to repeat herself so things will sink in. She claims she's forgotten everything. "After I lost those boys of mine, my head's so bad I can't remember a thing, a thing, a thing," she echoes. "I begged God to wipe my memory clean." And then she remembers everything, every single detail. What fifty-five-year-old Eva has lost is not her memory but her teeth. They've been rotting and falling out ever since her third son died. "That's that. I've lost everything. Everything died. Everything, everything, everything."

As she begins her tale of death, Eva says, "I've gone cold. I don't cry anymore. I don't feel anything anymore. Nothing, nothing, nothing." Then she starts crying and doesn't stop until the very end. The story of her life comes out drenched in tears. In Greek mythology, Zeus was moved by the wailing of Niobe, whose seven sons and seven daughters had been killed. In the legend, he turns the mother into a rock that spews water. This was how the ancients represented a pain devoid of any name. Mothers who lose their children to murder are weeping rocks.

Bloody Water on Tap

A dark spiral stairway takes you up to where Graça lives, on the top floor of a building occupied by squatters on the north side of Rio. Eight people are crowded into a two-room apartment with a tiny kitchen. The outside walls are pocked with bullet holes. Inside, Graça hears a cherry bomb and throws herself to the floor. Her grandchildren do the same. They think it's gunfire.

The young ones lost their fathers. She lost three sons, the last one a few months ago. When the five-year-old sleeps, his eyes stay half-open, and his body trembles in bed. When he wakes up, he has a vacant look. He himself is a cry for help, defeated before his time. A hopeless cry.

The police were accused of killing three boys from the building, kids in the drug trade. Their bodies were dumped down the spiral staircase, wrapped in black plastic. They bounced down the steps. One of them ended up in the water tank that supplies the building. Residents say the taps ran bloody for a while.

Graça remembers that the gunfire started blasting holes in the walls at eight in the morning. Her neighbor's son, a child, peeked out the window and nearly got hit. Bullets pierced the concrete. "The police came into my apartment. We were already on the floor. One of them put a rifle to my husband's head. They said they were going to kill him because his voice was annoying," she explains. "I crawled over to my husband and put my hand over his mouth. I had to drag myself. The kids were on the floor, clutching my leg."

She describes the country where she lives as broken in two. There's no visible, physical barrier between the favela and the surrounding city, only the snarled thoroughfare called Avenida Brasil. You'd think Graça could simply cross over. But the most insurmountable walls are precisely the ones you can't see. "We can't afford to move out of the favela. We're stuck here," she says. "Those that live on the outside don't know we live in a war zone. They don't even think we're human anymore. I'm so scared all the time. I wish I could hide under the ground. Under the ground. There I'd feel safe."

Graça is also losing her teeth.

A Rifle beside the Gate

One of the bagged bodies that was tossed down the spiral stairs was Josefa's son. Another was Francisca's. The blood flowing from the taps was from one of the boys. Francisca worked in Rio de Janeiro as a housemaid from the age of ten to forty-eight. She was never formally employed and never made the minimum wage. After she suffered a heart attack and had to stop working, she had no right to either a pension or disability. Her husband is a trash picker at a landfill. Her murdered son worked as a street cleaner, a butcher, and a vegetable delivery boy for a fresh food market. He even took a course to become a security guard. After a year without a job, he became a drug dealer. He lasted one year alive. "He earned seven hundred dollars a week. He paid for my medications and bus tickets, made the payments on my wardrobe, covered the gas bill, everything," says Francisca. "It wasn't what I wanted for him. I'd dreamed he'd be a mechanic. But I accepted his money because I had no choice."

When Josefa's son got home from work, he'd leave his weapon by the gate as if it were a toolbox. "Honey, I don't want those dangerous toys inside the house," Francisca would tell him. He obeyed like a good boy. While she made lunch, he'd shower. Francisca washed and mended his clothes and watched over his sleep. Only when the fireworks popped and banged in the favela, signaling the arrival of the police, was she forced to remember that the company her son worked for wasn't an ordinary one. Or legal.

One day he didn't come home. "I haven't been able to buy all my medications since he died. I fell behind on the payments for my glasses. Everything got real tough." Francisca recounts how her son died and begins to feel sick. She says it's her heart. Her daughter hurries to give her some medicine. "The people who live on the outside are scared of us. They think people from the favela are animals," the girl says. Francisca can't catch her breath.

In the narrow alleyways of the favela where Josefa and her daughter live, many young boys are growing up. Still skinny and awkward, no facial hair, all swagger, they wear shorts and baseball caps and carry the latest assault rifles in their hands. They have mothers who will bury them someday soon. They have sons who will replace them. The whole production line of the drug trade can be seen along a mere fifty-yard stretch of the alley, where filthy water pools beside mounds of trash. The boys who have died, the boys who have yet to die, the boys who will one day pick up a gun and die later—and the mothers who cry. All on the side of the city that supplies the other side, all on the side of the city where you get "murdered to death."

As the police leave the favela, at the invisible border between two worlds, they stop the news team. They're wielding AR-15s. They point them at the people getting out of the car, who are now suspects because they've been on the other side.

For a Dollar

"Oh my baby, mommy wants to dream about you," says Maria, a former factory worker, night after night. But she doesn't. Her son premiered in the drug trade at the age of twelve. He started out as an *avião*, a kid who does favors like delivering packages in exchange for drugs or money. By the time he was sixteen, his addiction was so bad he couldn't do the job. He couldn't be trusted anymore; he consumed the merchandise. He died at the age of twenty-five. He got into an argument with a drug dealer over the price of a rock of crack. Killed for a dollar.

"I did everything I could to save my son. When he started trashing the house, everybody fled, and I stayed. When he overdosed, I dragged him off the train tracks myself and put him in bed. When he was really high and buried his pistol in front of the other boys, I went over, dug it up, and threw it in the dealer's yard so my son wouldn't have any trouble later," says his mother. "I'd set food and fruit juice out in case he got hungry and managed to eat. I washed the underwear he soiled when the drugs gave him diarrhea. I hit him upside the head, yelled at him, checked him into a clinic. When I saw there was no getting around it, I fixed up a place at home just for him to do crack without anybody seeing, because I didn't have the money to get him out of jail."

Maria gathered her son up off the ground because no one else was brave enough to risk provoking his killer. "I took him to the hospital because I thought they could bring him back. I kept massaging him. I saw him take his last breath. Then I remembered it had been his dream to donate his organs. Only his kidneys and corneas could be used; the gunpowder had ruined the rest. It was one of those bullets that explode inside," she says. "If you lose your father or mother, it hurts a lot, but you get over it. If you lose a child, the wound never heals. My son came from my loins. I carried him nine months. I nursed him. I buried him."

Casket Number Two

The mother spent nearly five years paying for her son's casket. The boy was alive. Month after month, she tore a sheet out of the payment book: seven more dollars down. That's more than half of what she earns to wash, starch, and iron one bag of clothes. The boy was fifteen when she started paying off his death and twenty when she buried him, two weeks before Christmas. The day after that, she started buying a casket for her next son. He's nineteen and still alive—for now.

This saga of death sounds like something out of a horror story: the account of a mother who buys coffins for her healthy teenage boys, waiting to bury one after the other; the story of a mother driven to keep a deathwatch over the bodies of her living sons. The woman living out this saga is a diminutive forty-four-year-old who stands just four feet nine inches tall and resides on the urban periphery of Fortaleza, capital of Ceará. She is proof that reality can inflict a pain unknown in fiction.

Enilda is certain her second son will die soon, like the last one. "At the age of twelve, the older one was already using every drug in the world. His father beat him, I beat him. We gave him advice. It didn't do any good. I never accepted anything from him. I even turned him in to the police once. When he was twenty, I buried him, a bullet in his neck," she says. "Now I've got another going down the same path. He goes around biting his lips from so much powder. It's awful buying a casket for a son who's still alive, but my boys are going to die honorably."

The community has joined forces to welcome the news team to the favela where Enilda lives, ramshackle houses glued together in a row. A neighbor hurries to lend this reporter a chair, her best one. It has a nail in it. In the homes of the mothers whose sons have been killed in drug trafficking, the pain of death intertwines with the pain of life, weaving a story from the same spool of thread.

Enilda tells her tale beneath a ceiling fringed with bird cages. The chirruping of canaries and thrushes makes it hard to hear her. A much younger version of Enilda and her husband watches from a portrait on the wall, the kind where the photographer knocks on the door, takes a small snapshot of each person, and returns with a painted photograph. Enilda's husband looks like Brazilian actor Tony Ramos when he was young. She laughs hard when she hears this. As long as she's laughing, she isn't crying.

Enilda's only hope of finding peace is this motherly struggle to grant her dead sons a dignity they never had in life. If she couldn't find meaning in her act, she could never bear the insanity of pre-paying for her sons' six feet of ground, one after the other. Simple questions run through your mind at this point. How can she scrub, starch, and iron more than seventy pieces of clothing by hand to make only twelve dollars? How can her husband get up at three in the morning and bake bread until nighttime to earn just forty dollars a month? Isn't this the news story? Isn't the real report the fact that they ignore the explicit exploitation of their labor and their shameful living conditions, deciding instead to make honor their act of resistance?

Crime has divided their neighborhood on the periphery of Fortaleza into regions. The people living on one side can't go over to the other. If a man tries it, he's killed. If a woman does, she's stoned or beaten. One of the last men who dared defy this unwritten law crossed the bridge to help out a friend. First they executed him, then they urinated in his face. "I had to quit my studies because the school's on the other side, and I couldn't cross over," says Enilda's son's widow. "Now that he's dead, I've gone back." She spent a year carrying food to her incarcerated husband. She was pregnant when he was murdered, and she miscarried. She's just seventeen. Her life isn't measured in time. That's why her eyes are dead. "Dreams—I don't have any," she says. It's hard to look at her.

The mothers hustle their small children inside in the late after-noon, only opening the door the next day. Being locked up inside two windowless rooms in the tropical heat isn't easy. The sole bedroom in Enilda's house is shared by eight adults and children, plus over a dozen birds. Proportionately speaking, the thrushes enjoy more space than the people.

This is a common scenario on Brazil's poor urban peripheries, from north to south, where making children stay inside is an act of resistance. When they reach adolescence, it is an act of impotence. "We can keep a handle on them until they're ten or eleven. Then, overnight, you can't anymore," says Enilda. "And what's there for them outside? There's no entertainment, nothing. There's drug trafficking. Crack is destroying all the kids."

For Enilda, her son's life was more agonizing than his death. "I didn't want my son to die that horrible way. But I begged God he'd go to sleep and never wake up again. I couldn't take it anymore, watching the cops beat up my son. I asked them not to, but they did. He got a hernia in his testicles from being kicked so much," she says. "In his twenty years, he spent more time in prison than out."

After washing, starching, and ironing clothes, Enilda locks herself inside the house with her younger children. She watches every single soap opera on all the channels, from earliest to latest. Only then does she sleep. She wakes up in the middle of the night when she hears someone outside calling her: "Mom." She gets up and opens the door. "Nobody's ever there. My husband gets mad because I open the door. I go back to bed and cry till morning."

The Child Widow and the Next Generation

She's fourteen and a widow. Her baby is all that the oldest son of a greengrocer named Helena left behind. The girl was thirteen when she got pregnant and two months along at her husband's funeral. She went ahead with the pregnancy because the baby was wanted.

The child's father had spent years in prison. He was a crack addict and armed robber. The girl decided to get pregnant anyway. "I had the pill, condoms, injections. But I knew if I was carrying his baby, he wouldn't leave me. It was his dream to have a child," she says. "I thought he'd turn his life around, be a good father."

The girl belongs to the generation of child widows produced by the drug war. They get pregnant not because they don't know about birth control, but because they want to. An outlaw husband guarantees protection, support, and a better place to live than their parents' house, which is too often a battlefield. Having a baby is also a rite of passage that validates their position as women in the community. "I stayed with him because he was good for me. I had a calm life with him. It was a living hell at my mom's," she says. After the funeral, the young widow had to return to her mother's. Now she lovingly nurses her orphaned child.

In Brasilândia, a community in São Paulo, Eva watches for the arrival of another orphan, from atop the concrete slab of her rooftop. "My grandson might not come home one day. He's ten and already he doesn't like school. His father was murdered." Eva has stood lookout over the favela like this before, waiting for her three sons. And once, twice, three times, she waited in vain. When she spots her grandson's head as he ascends the steep street, Eva is glad to have one more day. And she cries over the empty landscape of tomorrow.

On the urban periphery of another Brazilian city, another grandson, raised by another grandmother, who is the mother of another murdered son, also waits. "I'm getting big, I'm getting real big," the boy says as he returns from school. "The guy that killed my dad was a coward. He's sixteen now. I miss my dad. I want him back." The boy is seven. He doesn't want to grow up to be a firefighter, a doctor, or a soccer player. He wants to grow up to kill another boy.

THE MIDDLE PEOPLE

Raimundo Nonato da Silva doesn't know who Luiz Inácio Lula da Silva is. Between the two da Silvas, the latter the president of Brazil and the former a Brazilian without a president, lies a vast world. Raimundo lives in a country unknown to Brazil itself, a land where most men answer to the name Raimundo. His republic lies in the heart of the Amazon and belongs to a region whose name sounds like it has been taken from J. R. R. Tolkien's mythological universe: Middle Earth. It's an invisible country because 99 percent of its inhabitants have no birth certificate or identification document. Officially, its Raimundos and Raimundas do not exist. But there they are, insisting on existing, shy on their ABCs, flush with paradoxes. Illiterate or, as they put it, "blind." They've never voted because phantoms only become voters before the ends of the earth, and they reside after the earth ends. The Middle People might vanish before their official country even notices them. Like the forest where they live, and with which they merge, they're an endangered species.

The Middle People are descendants of the "rubber soldiers" known as *arigós*, who were drawn from the Northeast to the far reaches of the jungle by the Getúlio Vargas administration during World War II. There they settled and multiplied, eventually forming a single family of fewer than two hundred people entwined in an intricate web of kinships. They live like the Indians did before having contact with what is called civilization. As hunters and gatherers, they eat what the forest gives them, and it gives them a lot: Brazil nuts in the winter; game, fish, and oil from the copaiba and andiroba trees year round.

They would have gone on with their lives like this, in their country without a currency, had they not been discovered by the men known as *grileiros*, or land-grabbers. As predators who are old acquaintances of the Amazon, the *grileiros* send in their gunmen, armed and with licenses to kill. Brandishing land deeds forged within a network of corruption that spreads into notary public offices and government agencies, these men proclaim themselves owners of thousands, even millions of acres of forest. Few of them appear to be what they are. Most live in big cities in the Brazilian South, Southeast, or Central-West and rely on front men to commit their crimes, while they, nails buffed, attend classical music concerts.

As in the days of Pedro Álvares Cabral, the representatives of *grileiros* first offered the Raimundos small trinkets—in this case, a fistful of Brazilian *reais*—to leave the forest. Then they showed them the barrels of their shotguns. Today the Middle People have been marked for death. One man alone, Cecílio do Rego Almeida, owner of a large construction firm and one of the few land-grabbers in Brazil whose face is known, is fighting in court over an area that may exceed seventeen million acres, a territory the size of the Netherlands and Belgium combined. If he wins, he'll force all of the Middle People off their lands.

"The only way they'll drag me out of here is with a gun to my head," says Raimundo Belmiro, thirty-nine, father of nine children. Raimundo, one of the community leaders, is a quiet man with the courage of someone who does what his character tells him, heedless of fear. "I came back from the woods one day and the outsiders were in my home. Then others came, and they never stopped coming. They offered me $3,500 for my land. I turned it down. Next they started coming at my place from all sides. They go by on the river in *rabetas*, small motorized canoes, full of armed gunmen. They've got reliable rapid-fire weapons, not like my twenty-three-year-old shotgun. They want to scare me. And they do. I've been marked for death."

Raimundo and his family had woken up that morning with nothing to eat. Each of them pushed into the bush in a different cardinal direction in search of food. Before noon, Fernando, thirteen, had taken down a tapir that weighed over 650 pounds, while Francisco, fourteen, brought back two peccaries. Raimundo explains: "That's the forest, rich in everything. That's why I've been marked for death. But I stay."

A Country of Raimundos

Raimundo's story is a replay of the story of Chico Mendes, promoted to national hero following a murder foretold, but prevented by no one. Yet Raimundo's world lies even deeper in the forest. Covering nearly twenty million acres, Middle Earth offers one of the very last chances to preserve the Amazon. Embedded in the state of Pará, the region earned its name because it lies entrenched between the Xingu and Iriri Rivers. Surrounded by indigenous territories and national forests, Middle Earth's geographical whereabouts have long protected it from devastation—official, in the form of numerous predatory attempts to occupy the jungle, especially by military governments, and private, led by predators in the guise of entrepreneurs, who employ the pretty word *agribusiness*. This no-man's-land is claimed by many.

In the 1990s, the *grileiros* ramped up their border assault through the poaching operations of the mahogany mafia. A decade later, news about the paving of the Trans-Amazonian and Cuiabá-Santarém Highways has heightened the pressure. To the southeast, around the town of São Félix do Xingu, the region has become a Wild West. Most of the cases of slave labor, illegal logging, and deaths caused by the land disputes that feed the national news occur here. Along the northeastern border, where the city of Altamira stands as gateway, the invasion advances apace. It is to the northwest, on the banks of Anfrísio's Little River, that an entire population of Raimundos lives, every home lying hours or even days away from others by canoe.

The river's name is derived from Anfrísio Nunes, a man from the state of Sergipe, who, like so many others, received government authorization to exploit the Amazon's rubber trees. His descendants also claim ownership of the land. "Anfrísio brought more than two hundred families of *arigós* from the Northeast to tap rubber along the Little River," says his stepdaughter and daughter-in-law, Vicencia Meirelles Nunes, seventy-four. "Back then, the Indians decimated entire families of *arigós*. Anfrísio raised eighteen orphans of people who'd been killed by the Caiapó or Arara."

These Raimundos are the people who descended from the *arigós*. Left to fend for themselves once rubber was no longer profitable, they molded their destinies far from the presence of the State, without schools, health care, or birth certificates. They don't want to own the forest, just live in it. Their worldview does not include fences.

Herculano's Journey

To show Brazil that his people exist, a slight man named Herculano Porto, sixty years old, was chosen to travel to Altamira. As the sole head of household who possesses any documents, this man with the profile of a bird and eyes of a cat was the only one of the Middle People suited to undertake the journey, and he became the community's president. After rowing his canoe for a day, he reached the mouth of Anfrísio's Little River, and from there took a motorboat. Along the way, he came upon a jaguar that was crossing the river. "We thought it was a deer and drove the boat right over it," he says.

It was September 7, Brazilian Independence Day, when Herculano began his return trip. He had accomplished his mission. He carried back with him two soccer balls and a document drawn up by the Catholic Church's Pastoral Land Commission, in which the community asked the federal government to create an extractive reserve. At the bottom of the petition, his people would have to record their thumbprints as signatures.

Between Herculano and his country, which is accessible only by boat, stretch 204 miles of waterways. His saga would only come to a close several days later, at the end of a tapestry of rivers leading steadily inland. After leaving the Xingu, the Iriri penetrates deep into Middle Earth over a labyrinth of rocks. Travelers have to conquer half a dozen rapids, getting out at each one and portaging upstream, where they drop their boat back into the current by rope. The task tears their hands until they bleed.

Schooled in the language of water, Herculano had no fear of the river's traps. The only thing that vexed him was the counsel of his boatman, Benedito dos Santos, who in his sixty-two years of Amazonian life has been a rubber tapper, prospector, pimp, jaguar hunter, and hired gun. There's not a story he tells in which two or three men don't die. "I've run a lot of people off land for the big guys in this Amazon. It's easier to handle things with violence. This story's been repeated over and over, and I've never seen a settler win. The world will always have fights over land," he says, spinning his tales down the river. "Hey guy, sell your parcel fast before they throw you off it!" Herculano gives a little grin lacking in teeth but brimming with perseverance.

It takes seven days by passenger boat to reach the mouth of Herculano's country during the dry season—if all goes well. Passengers often have to camp alongside trickier stretches for weeks until they can be conquered. Along the way, men like Herculano probe the river and woodlands in search of food, especially a type of turtle known as a *tracajá*. The forest is their restaurant.

At the close of day, after the sun has gone down and the rocks on the river bottom have become invisible and lethal, the men eat their only meal. They bathe in the waters, dragging their feet along the bottom, careful not to step on a ray armed with a venomous dagger. A few yards away, the flashlight eyes of caimans peer out, waiting for some careless soul to venture a bit closer. Herculano and his folk don't take any chances. They belong to this world, they are nature. They tie their hammocks to the trees and stretch out for a night of murmurous sleep.

In the wee hours of these nights, the silence of the forest is made up of noises. Herculano Porto knows each by name; he has the forest inside his head. The animals don't attack. Since the ecosystem is still in balance, there's food for everyone and humans are predators that not even jaguars challenge without a strong reason. In the water, only anacondas devour people, like creatures from a nearly lost world. Not long after Herculano passed through on this particular journey, one of these snakes killed a man who was out swimming. It crushed his bones and then swallowed him whole.

While Herculano was sailing the rivers of his primitive world, the Sofazenda real estate agency, based in Varginha, Minas Gerais, was offering part of his land on the internet for three million dollars. The ad proclaimed the wonders of Anfrísio's Little River: "Dozens of types of hardwood stand in thick forests filled with mahogany," along with "large deposits of ore, cassiterite, gold, diamonds, and the like." When he was contacted, the real estate agent Aldamir Rennó Pinto explained that the area had been removed from their catalog "because things got held up." He offered another tract, of 950,000 acres, for nine million dollars. "In fact, the other land was inside this one that I'm offering you now. It belongs to Anfrísio Nunes's heirs and I've already got the titles, all in order."

Herculano, who is illiterate, confronts the universe of cybernetic land-grabbing with the blows of his thumbprint. When he finally landed back home, he found that his grove of Brazil nut trees had been razed. The only thing left was to fell the biggest trees and then set them afire. For Herculano, a nut grove holds the past, present, and future. It is almost the mirror of a man.

Likewise marked to die, Herculano had accomplished his mission. But when the document bearing his people's fingerprints finally reaches the official country, in Brasilia, no one there will have any notion of how enormous his odyssey was.

The Dispute over Souls

Before the invaders arrived, Middle Earth had functioned without money. Then land-grabbers brought in currency and covetousness, penetrating cracks in souls and dividing to sow discord. Francisco dos Santos, the man most familiar with the river and its whims, was the first to be assailed by temptation. Chico Preto, as Santos is known, sold himself for seven dollars a day, bringing workhands and gunmen in and out of the region of Anfrísio's Little River. "I fight for the reserve, but they pay on time and it's tough to make money here any other way," says Chico. "They're cheerful folks, obliging, doesn't even seem like they'd kill people."

Chico's stepson, yet another Raimundo, became right-hand man to a land-grabber known as Goiano, legendary for the atrocities he has committed. At the mouth of the river, he works the radio that warns when strangers are arriving. "Better to sell the land, because they're going to take it anyway. Then they kick us off empty-handed," argues this dissident Raimundo.

Taking advantage of government neglect, the land-grabbers offer what the State doesn't. "I want to improve things for these people. A school and a clinic. I've made sure there's a car at their disposal," says Edmilson Teixeira Pires, who claims ownership of a few dozen square miles. He has already cut in a road, off the Trans-Amazonian Highway, where he put up more than one house and dozens of workhands. He failed to reach the river solely because his path was blocked by Luiz Augusto Conrado, known as Streak in honor of the lock of gray hair he has sported since infancy. "You can back right up. On my land, you guys don't set foot," he warned.

Streak is quite familiar with the loving-kindness displayed by the big guys. Before marrying Francineide, a midwife from Anfrísio's Little River, he was a slave on large farms and ranches in Pará for more than ten years. Then he was a prospector in Serra Pelada. He's seen everything except enough gold to change his fortune. He knows full well what his resistance is made of: "The forest is the only place where there's abundance for the poor. The man starts fencing us in, and we need Brazil nuts, game, fish. They're killing us off because they're shrinking the land. When just one of those roads that they're cutting in here reaches the river, that'll be the end of us and the forest."

Targeted for Extinction

If the invaders win, the forest will vanish, along with 346 species of trees, 1,398 types of vertebrates, and 530 kinds of fish. A good share of these varieties are endogenous, found nowhere but in Middle Earth. The world will be poorer in biodiversity—poverty of an irreparable sort. Besides losing thousands of species, the planet will also be less varied in people. The Middle People are among the last of their breed, mowed down along with the forest. In the far reaches of Brazil, isolation has produced the extravagance of an imageless culture that has persisted into the twenty-first century.

This is why it has become a land of Raimundos. With no television to watch, these people never name their children after foreign celebrities, transcribing Michael as "Maicon" or Jennifer as "Dienifer," nor have they heard that João and Maria are now stylish names elsewhere in Brazil. They are devotees of Saint Raymond Nonnatus, who was pulled from his dead mother's womb and so became the protector of midwives when he reached sainthood. Their social imagination is pieced together entirely by ear, its visions drawn from bits and pieces broadcast by Rádio Nacional da Amazônia, their only contact with Brazil. This is how they reinvent soccer plays, from moves they hear but never see.

Ronaldo and Ronaldinho Gaúcho are faceless idols, their feats reinterpreted in the mind of each Raimundo. Soccer is how these men of the forest earn their Brazilian IDs. Their identity is the ball, traded for 440 pounds of Brazil nuts at the *regatão*, a kind of floating shopping market that stops by half a dozen times a year so people can barter local products for merchandise from the city.

Raimundo Nonato da Silva, the Brazilian who doesn't know who Lula is, has a soccer field across from his wattle-and-daub house, roofed with palm fronds. On Sundays his boys swap their tapping knives for the ball. It is at this dirt-floor notary office that they register their births. "It'd be nice to know the name of the president of Brazil just to know it, but it doesn't make any difference," their father says.

Anyone unfamiliar with Raimundo's lot in life might think he's a bit touched in the head. Heir to a rubber soldier who dropped dead among the trees—"My dad's name was Zuza, last name Zé"—he has lived a Stateless life since he was born. All he knows is that beyond the river lies a place called "city," which he enigmatically conceives of as "a kind of movement." For him, the name of the president really doesn't matter. The idea of country has no place in his social imagination. It is Brazil who needs to discover Raimundo, before it's too late.

THE VOICE

Clodair can't see his hand in front of his face. Nor can he see his face. Can't see a thing. But to make up for it, what a voice! Piercing as a tenor's high C, mighty as a tuba. And with a very, very long reach. It's a voice like Cauby Peixoto's:

Conceição! I remember so well . . .

He's a Brazilian Tom Jones belting out "Delilah."

This Cauby voice has become the scourge of Rua da Praia, at the intersection of Ladeira Street, in downtown Porto Alegre. Just imagine Cauby, from seven forty-five to ten in the morning, Tuesdays to Saturdays.

"Meeeega-Seeeena Jackpot! Ten million dollar rollover! Get your ticket now!"

On and on and on. Six hundred and seventy-eight times.

He's not exactly a hit with either the public or critics.

It's been a war. A blind one, true enough, but never deaf or dumb, and this war has reached a perilous point. Clodair Cauby plants himself perpendicular to the Monteiro Lobato course, which offers high school equivalency classes and prepares students for the college entrance exam, and shoots his vocal cannon into the heavens. On the second floor, Bruno Eizerik, the course director, talks on the phone to an ad agency in São Paulo.

"What's going on there in Porto Alegre? What kind of demonstration is that?" asks the clueless fellow on the other end of the line.

"It's that blind guy," grumbles Bruno. "That blind guy!"

On the sixth floor, Pinheiro Eizerik, founder of the course, tries to combat the blast rising up, and up, and up, by tuning in to a Tchaikovsky concert on public radio. He tries. His Philips radio shudders, but the result is at most a fusion of Tchaikovsky and Clodair Cauby. Tchaikovsky and "Get your jackpot ticket for one dollar!"

"I've failed," he says.

Eizerik is a Napoleon at his Waterloo. His dismay rises as the intonation falls. On the eighth floor, Evelise Bernardes, a prep course student, leaves aside the mysteries of adversative conjunctions. She's about to commit a reckless act, resort to madness, to outright evil. Evelise wants to torture the blind fellow, and make herself enemy number one of human rights organizations, defenders of the disadvantaged. She scribbles in her notebook in a trance, like Jack Nicholson's character in *The Shining*.

From 6:40 a.m. to 10:45 a.m., he hollered nonstop:
"Millionaire jackpot!"
"Drawing today!"
"Ten thousand dollars!"
"Millionaire jackpot draws today!"
"Jackpot rollover draws today!"
"Ten thousand dollar draw today!"

Evelise enrolled in the course last August and has become the commander in chief of its anti–blind man brigade. All because, as a greenhorn, she had once decided to march down to the street and ask Clodair Cauby if he couldn't kindly yell a little softer. Clodair Cauby didn't appreciate the sudden interruption of his artistic expression, and he brandished—only brandished—a cane that has been known for a while downtown. It looks like a cane, acts like a cane, has cane written all over it. But it's a weapon. A metal weapon. To tell the truth, Clodair Cauby, in his zeal to defend his *modus vivendi*, also got a bit unpublishable.

Evelise concluded that it would be much, much worse than failing her law school entrance exam to retake the prep course with Clodair Cauby around.

Evelise, the new owner of a set of puffy bags under her eyes, sent a poignant petition to the Ninth Battalion of the Military Police. In it, she reported on the "collective neurosis" that hits the students whenever Clodair Cauby releases the gift that God gave him to make up for what he took.

"He's subjecting us to psychological torture! He attacks us with curse words! He swings his cane around!" Evelise vents.

This is grave, very grave.

So grave that some students have contemplated doing a remake of a Hitchcock classic. They've thought about sprinkling Clodair Cauby with pigeon food and leaving him to the eager beaks of birds. They've thought of other things. They've thought of . . . well, better not go there.

For his part, when he's approached about the topic, Clodair José Pinheiro Maidana, Clodair Cauby, rolls his eyes in a sign of superiority. His voice rises above these mundane matters. About nine floors above them, at least. He's a guy from Alegrete. Forty-two years old. A fan not of Cauby Peixoto but of the fifties band Renato and His Blue Caps. Father to a boy and a girl. Resident of Leopoldina. Defender (of course) on his bell ball soccer team. He makes around twelve dollars for a three-hour day, Tuesday to Saturday.

"I'll only leave here if they pay me sixty dollars a month. Or if they give me a job as a phone operator at the course."

Period. A few steps away from Clodair Cauby, his wife, Eva,

whom he met at one of the dances put on by the Santa Luzia Institute for the Blind, has a percussion voice. Like a triangle. She sings backup.

"I can't go against my husband," she explains, all tinny.

She swears he doesn't holler at home. Much.

The voice is now a police case filed at the Seventeenth Precinct. It's made its way through the courts. During a hearing at the Third Criminal Court, Clodair Cauby promised he'd yell "more softly."

Clodair Cauby just can't tone it down. He likes to do a job well. Give free rein to his deeper self. Sing out good fortune to the people, from one end of Rua da Praia to the other. He's popular up and down the whole street. Everyone knows him—him, his voice, and his cane.

"Ugh! Don't tell me it's the blind guy bellowing! I'm outta here!"

A fellow tradesman with the voice of João Gilberto—delightful hours can be spent listening to him sing out the Mega-Sena to a bossa nova beat—thinks he could actually restrain Clodair's big voice, but he'd rather not go head-to-head with his buddy. Or side to side. Or any way at all. Considering that even the clown who occasionally cavorts around there had some of the fun caned out of him . . .

No one knows how the story will finally end. Although people on the street are wagering on Clodair Cauby ten to zero.

For now, the ending goes like this:

At 10:00 a.m. on the dot, Clodair Cauby and his wife meet at an invisible spot midway between the ten steps that separate them, lock arms, and walk off down the street, canes in hand.

High up in the building, 450 students lean out the window and breathe a sigh of joy. They stop short of shouting "Hurrah!"

Down below, Clodair stretches his booming Cauby voice and remarks to his wife: "You know, Eva, you can't imagine the headache I get from hollering like that."

JOÃO ASKS RAIMUNDA TO
DIE WITH HIM IN SACRIFICE

The saga of João and Raimunda comes to a head against the back-drop of a massacre acknowledged neither by the Brazilian government nor by most Brazilians. As their two-act drama unfolds, it is in the forest that they search for a way out, swept along by the current of the Xingu, one of the Amazon's most biodiversified rivers. And there they find their futures, like the river, dammed up. A man and a woman, just two among the thousands forced out by the construction of Belo Monte, planned to be the world's third-largest hydro-electric project. Today, João and Raimunda, refugees from their own country, wander a territory they no longer recognize and where they do not recognize themselves. Their bodies bear the imprint of a historic crossroads, of a country that has reached the present after belonging to the future for so very long, only to find itself mired in the past. Their story is the epilogue of a political party elected to power on the promise that it would deliver dignity to the poorest and most vulnerable, but that betrayed them, here in the region farthest from the center of Brazil's political and economic power. Their story also reveals the anatomy of a distortion: that of living in a formal democracy while subject to powers above the law. When victims suffer violence that goes unacknowledged, it inflicts even greater pain on them, and they are violated all over again by a feeling of unreality. When their world convulsed, Raimunda and João chose different destinies.

Raimunda opted to live, even though she was shattered to pieces. João doesn't know how to live. For him, meaning lies solely in sacrifice through death.

João and Raimunda have arrived at this impasse.

Act 3 is still an uncertainty.

ACT 1

João Loses His Speech and Locks Up His Legs to Keep from Committing Murder

On Monday, March 23, 2015, João Pereira da Silva stood before a representative of Norte Energia, the consortium that won the bid for Belo Monte Dam. He was hoping to receive a fair market value for his house and fields, which were located on the island from which the dam had expelled him. Instead, Norte Energia established a price of $7,250, not enough to purchase a piece of property where João could once again earn a living by planting, fishing, and harvesting products from the forest. He realized he was condemned to poverty at the age of sixty-three. The law didn't hold in his case. From the age of eight, João had traversed different Brazils in search of a plot of land without an owner, wrenching a living from the strength of his arms. After a journey of wants, he thought he'd found a home and a life free from hunger on the island of Xingu. Now they had wrested him from there as well. He felt they were robbing him of his life and that he was neither young enough nor healthy enough to begin again. There was no final frontier for João, in a country nearly the size of a world. He no longer had legs to walk on. Everything had been taken from him, even meaning itself. As far as he was concerned, the past-present-future had been reduced to a single tense, repeating itself over and over. And on every new morning, João found his legs bound to a frozen minute hand, tethered to a place that wasn't.

João wanted to kill the man standing before him. Not out of revenge, he explains, but as a form of sacrifice.

"If I was to do damage to some big guy, some big guy inside there, maybe it'd make things better for others. I'd be sacrificing my own life, but other people's lives would be better. If I could, I'd give it to the company's biggest boss, I'd give it to him a couple hundred times. And I'm not afraid of saying it: I'd be mighty pleased to do it, even if my life was to end right then and there."

João was unable to commit the deed. His urge to kill didn't turn into action. He discovered it was impossible for him to do it. His legs locked up and so did his speech. João stilled his whole self to keep from murdering the man who embodied the project that had just killed him. Instead, he made a sacrifice of himself. He had to be carried out of the office by his wife, Raimunda, and one of their daughters.

"I lost—it got to the point where I lost my voice. I lost everything. I just sputtered. And my nerves locked everything all up. Locked up so tight I couldn't walk. I can walk a bit now, but my legs ache, and they swell up. It's not easy to get so angry that your body locks up."

João has been traumatized ever since. Not the watered-down sense of "traumatic," something merely upsetting, but the sense of "trauma" as something that cannot be symbolized, of a wound that does not heal. Not knowing where to go, or even where he is, João manages to walk only a few steps and then needs to sit down on a stool. He gets lost when he goes out because he doesn't recognize where he is. João has been exiled from everything, including himself. Several days ago, a friend called up Raimunda to say, "João's sitting in the middle of nowhere, in the sun. He's going to die out there." Raimunda asked one of their daughters to rescue him.

If João had been able to talk that day, what would he have said?

"I would've said a lot. The first thing is that there's no justice in 'the Brazilian country.'"

João pauses before explaining.

"You've got to understand something. It wasn't about talking, but about doing. Those people turn my stomach. God forgive me, but they do."

Wordless and deedless, João is the victim of a catastrophe. He is a victim twice over, because his country doesn't acknowledge the catastrophe. So João also becomes country-less. He has the abysmal sensation that he is inside and outside at the same time, affected by unwritten laws and ignored by the laws that should grant him his place in the realm of citizenship. When he's referring to Brazil, João most often uses the expression "the Brazilian country." In this choice of words, Brazil is a body to which he does not belong. And so João is condemned like a pariah.

"I said it before and I'll say it again. I'll say it to [President] Dilma [Rousseff], I'll say it to God, Satan, and any dog who comes round: in the Brazilian country, money is justice. If Jesus shows up here in this country, the big businessmen will hunt him down and buy him. And if he's dumb about it, he'll get sold. Understand?"

João repeats the one-word question "Understand?" over and over. After listening to him for a while, you realize it's not a linguistic crutch, but rather his certainty that he will not be understood.

ACT 2

Raimunda Discovers Her Home Has Turned to Ashes

On Tuesday, September 1, 2015, Raimunda Gomes da Silva, fifty-six, called an acquaintance, bought ten liters of gasoline for their trip on the river, and fixed a "little lunch box, with some fried food" to eat on the way to her island of Barriguda, in the area christened Furo do Pau Rolado. They left at five in the morning. The day before, the people from Norte Energia had phoned: "Mrs. Silva, when can we get your leftovers off the island?" Her "leftovers" were Raimunda's kitchen things and fishing gear. They arranged for her to pick up her belongings early Tuesday. After two and a half hours on the river, Raimunda reached the island.

Her house, built of resistant acapu lumber, was still burning.

"You know, my friend, to tell you the truth, I got out of the boat and didn't feel the ground. I didn't feel the earth under my feet because that just made my mind go blank. Right there at that moment, I don't know what I felt. Because when I looked at it from far away, I didn't think . . . when we got there and I saw my home burned, I got out, went up the bank, sat down, and I went blank, erased, I don't know. I don't even know how to tell you what I know, what I felt, I don't know, because I didn't feel anything . . . I was numbed by what I saw. I mean, how could they call to tell me to get what was mine and then burn the whole house down the day before? I stood there frozen, just thinking about life, you know. What world is this we're living in?"

The company in charge of building the hydroelectric dam didn't consider Raimunda's house a house. They told her it was a *tapiri*, a hut. Raimunda retorted, "In your language, sir, it might be all of that. But in mine, it's my house. And I felt fine in it." When she found her home in ashes, Raimunda sat down on the riverbank.

"I never thought they'd set fire to it. If I set fire to their office, I'd spend the rest of my life in prison. They set fire to my home and nothing happens. This is the prophecy of the end of the world that my father talked about, the big wheel passing through the smaller one."

She ends with these words:

"They're certain they can do whatever they want and never be punished. Maybe I'm not certain in what I say. But they know what they do."

Raimunda looked for her Buddha belly plant, which stood in front of her house.

"This shrub was my main friend. Because that's what I believed. If I came out here early in the morning and its leaves were limp and droopy, I wouldn't go out on the river that day. Because it was telling me something, in its language. It was trying to protect me from something. But if it was all perky, then I knew everything was fine with me."

Raimunda looked for her "main friend" but it was already something that wasn't.

"Now I've got no one left to guide me."

So Raimunda sings beside the ashes.

"It's really difficult to see what's yours all burned up. The only way I can express myself is by singing. So my plants will know that I never wanted them to be burned. So they feel I'm here. Since they don't know how to talk, and I don't know the language of the plants, I sing to them. I tell them the world doesn't end here because my house is burned. The world is still standing. For as long as God gives me life, I'll carry this with me: hope and faith. I tell them that one day justice will be real. Because right now, justice is an apparition, a myth. They say it exists, but poor people never see it."

The Before

Raimunda's Father Teaches Her to Walk without Making a Sound

Raimunda parades down the hall in her rubber sandals. "Look, I can walk in any shoes without making a sound," she says.

I make a joke only a white woman who has read a lot of fairy tales would make: "The walk of a princess, right, Raimunda?"

She fires back at me: "The walk of someone who's spent her life working in other people's homes."

Raimunda's father is her foundation. She repeats his lessons while she describes the disintegration of her world, as if the former could repair the gash in the latter. Natalino Gomes was the great-grandson of slaves, a man whose very voice exuded pain. The cinnamon of his Indian grandmother spiced his African blood.

"My great-grandfather passed the shackles down to my grandfather, who passed them down to my father, and so on. He never stopped being a slave, my father, because the only thing he knew was how to work for others. He didn't know how to deal with the business of money or how to read. My father taught all his children not to make a sound when they walked. I was raised in the culture of 'yes sir, no sir.' But I never did get used to it."

Perhaps Raimunda inherited her fire from her mother, Maria Francisca Gomes. She was a *mãe de santo*, a high priestess in the Afro-Brazilian religion of Candomblé. Her mother defied her father's Catholicism, the religion forced on black people under slavery. Maria was happy. She was free, as Raimunda puts it. As free as poverty allows. Free to live other realities, beyond shackles. Her mother was also feisty. She wouldn't let any man put a yoke on her, not even her husband—especially not her husband. She worked as a babassu coconut breaker, off to her labor every day, a gaggle of boys flocking around her. Raimunda has carried coconuts since she was five and split them open with a hatchet since she was seven. Her hands hold the scars of this trade that has mutilated so many children, slicing off fingers and futures. But this was before she ambled off with her velvet footsteps to work in other people's homes at the age of ten. She taught herself to read, joining one letter to another to see what happened. She was a stranger to school.

Raimunda tells me: "My mind's my own, it's what I speak."

And then she does.

"Slavery isn't over, it's just disguised. Slavery's still here, down and dirty. It comes in a different model, but it's here. Because that's what being a slave is. Not having any rights. Did you see what happened to me and thousands of others because of this Belo Monte? And where's justice? There it is, a heap of injustices in the face of justice. So, I'm a slave."

Raimunda thinks she has left too much unsaid and decides to speak her whole mind:

"Black people always come in the second part of history. Or maybe the third. Never the first."

If shackles restrained the silent steps of Raimunda's father, Natalino, he still had his dreams. And it was because of these dreams, this flicker of hope coursing through the veins of Brazilians, that he moved his family from the dry hinterlands of Maranhão state to the Amazon of waters. Natalino was pursuing land for someone who had nothing at a time when Brazil's civil-military dictatorship was marketing the forest as "a land without men for men without land," given that Indians were not considered people. Natalino didn't get his land, and this is why Raimunda says her father died a slave. In the Amazons of Pará, Raimunda continued to work as a nanny and maid in other people's homes.

Raimunda's father bequeathed her a series of sayings and some prophecies as well. Recalling one of these, she draws bridges between the slavery of the past and the slavery of the present, between banishment from one continent to another, and banishment within banishment.

"My father used to say that someday the world would be moved by paper. And here it is, money. Isn't that what happened? Belo Monte came along giving orders, tearing things down, crushing them, and tossing out those scraps of paper, the money they hand out. They don't see how they've wiped out the person inside when they take his house. Understand? They take everything the person has and toss him some bits of paper. Understand?"

Like her husband, João, Raimunda completes her sentences with the word *understand*. But her *understand* has a different meaning. Raimunda believes she can still be understood, and she demands to be. Her interrogative is a knife at her listener's throat.

She continues like a blade.

"Nobody lives off money. Go get lost in the forest with a bag full of money and see how much it's worth: nothing! But spend some time lost in the forest without a bag full of money and you'll manage to survive. You find a plant, you find some fruit, you drink some water. The forest offers you everything you need to stay alive until someone finds you. But you'll die with money on your back. It's worthless."

Raimunda clings to the ground of her father's words. No one can tear her off this symbolic land. And since catastrophe had been predicted by her father, the one whose feet dragged shackles, she has the brutal feeling everything lies beyond any control, but this doesn't paralyze her. "Paper has finished off the world, like my father said. He knew." Her father also said, "Follow the trails." Raimunda always figures out a way to find a trail.

The Before
Abandoned by His Father, João Lives on the Trecho *and Works as a Dam Builder*

João was also born in Maranhão, but the state is not a land of belonging for him. João didn't migrate like Raimunda. He became a migrator. His father caught a fever much worse than the ague of malaria, one that lasts much longer, and sometimes kills too: gold fever.

The idea of striking it rich and finding so much gold that poverty becomes nothing but a dusty photograph is what moves the hearts of thousands, perhaps millions, of men all over Brazil. Every time a new glittery vein is hit, they rush to the site by boat, by bus, crowded into the back of a pickup truck, on foot, with little more than the clothes on their backs and a fierce dream. This is their way of refusing to have but one lot in life—poverty—preferring to lead a life of adventure and consumption. A life, as one prospector put it, like a "character in a book." When he made this remark, he forgot that he didn't know how to read.

As usual in Brazil, a country where a person's place in life is bound by the unfinished abolition of slavery, the poor are criminalized whenever they reject their fate and raise their heads to peer at the horizon. Prospectors are treated like criminals, while big mining companies and multinationals, the ones that raze vast stretches of the forest to amass profit, are purified by labels like "business," "enterprise," and "development."

João's father was one of those feverish men who abandoned his family, including his young son, to consume himself in his inner El Dorado. He had some land in the Northeast and even a few head of cattle but he wasn't a man with roots. He ventured into the prospecting sites of Itaituba, in Pará, where the Brazilian government is now clearing the way for two other major hydroelectric dams in the Amazon forest: São Luiz do Tapajós and Jatobá. Like most prospectors, he found himself a new woman there, possibly several.

The prostitutes generally beat the prospectors to the sites, or at least arrive around the same time. They are known as "free women" and they work under assorted arrangements. In exchange for a predetermined amount of gold, set in grams, a woman might agree to belong to one man alone, living with him in the prospecting village, cooking, washing his clothes, and sleeping with him, as if she were his wife. Sometimes, she might become his wife. When João's father returned for his son, thinking to take him back to the mining region, it was too late for a relationship that had never been. His father tried twice. One time he even showed up in a plane. João had no faith in his father's wings and refused to follow him. He preferred to make himself into a man while still a boy.

When João was eight, a wisp of a lad, he worked in fields that belonged to some of his relatives. At twelve he broke loose, hazarding a life on the *trecho*, one of the most enigmatic words in the diverse languages of multiple Brazils, a word whose meaning changes with the region. The *trecho* is the world, the road, life in movement, an elsewhere pregnant with possibility. João lived on the *trecho*, working hard, lugging more rocks than he could, inventing muscles before he had any, because a poor, unlettered boy has to sustain his life by the might of his limbs. He'd been condemned by his father, who said: "A boy's school is the handle of a hoe, or of a machete."

João didn't take up mining. That had been his father's choice, but João didn't think of himself as his father's son anymore. He preferred to bind his own ties. Among the lots assigned to poor Brazilians, he chose the life of a *barrageiro*, a laborer who goes from dam to dam, following the trail of major government projects. When there's no power plant to be built, *barrageiros* sign contracts to work outside the country for one of Brazil's construction giants. João unfurls the names of big contractors whose government connections were as tight under the dictatorship as they are under democracy. "I worked for Mendes Júnior, for Queiroz Galvão, for Camargo Corrêa, for Odebrecht, for Andrade Gutierrez, for Constran, for Construpar. I worked for some other miserable little companies. I know I worked for about twelve construction firms."

João was a pawn in a game of chess where the Amazon and Brazil were the board. In the 1950s, under the democratic government of Juscelino Kubitschek, contractors built Oscar Niemeyer's and Lúcio Costa's modernist new capital, Brasilia, and never again vacated the center of political power. They grew and multiplied their profits shortly thereafter with the big projects of the civil-military dictatorship (1964–1985), particularly its megalomaniac works in the Amazon, like the Trans-Amazonian Highway, one of many endeavors that destroyed forests and lives. Following the money of

Brazil's big construction companies means negotiating at least sixty years of the country's history, from the latter half of the twentieth century to the first fifteen years of the twenty-first.

In the early days of his life as a *barrageiro*, João was a simple laborer. Then he learned a trade as an operator of heavy machinery. His first large hydroelectric project was Itaipu, in Paraná, the Brazilian-Paraguay dam that drowned Seven Falls, one of the wonders of the world. But it was only at another dam, Tucuruí, that João came to understand the disposable role he played in a game ruled by kings, and later by a queen. At the moment he discovered this, João was beginning the definitive chapter of his life, alongside Raimunda.

Marriage
João and Raimunda Meet at a Dance Party

Raimunda was sixteen when she met João at a dance. "It was a big party," she explains. "I looked at him, and he looked me back." And so it was, between the blue tint of João's eyes and the black tint of Raimunda's, that they wanted one another at first sight. Raimunda was quick to tell him: "I don't come from a tradition where people live together. If you want me, give me a ring and a last name, and we'll make history." They did. They made it official at a collective wedding ceremony some time later. Raimunda dressed up in lilac, according to her, a "woman's color." After that, they inaugurated a line of daughters, seven girls in all, every name beginning with the letter *L*. And just one son, baptized Leodeí, who died of meningitis when he was seventeen months old.

"I worked at this lady's home, and she had a son in the army. He died in a town called Indonesia. I kept that name in my head, Indonesia . . . the mother's dream was to visit the town because her son had died and stayed over there. Years later, they brought back his remains, but it wasn't her son anymore. I kept thinking to my-self: If Indonesia is a town that a war was waged on, a pointless war, and it's at peace now, I want my daughter to have this name. So I named her Lindionésia. And then came Lindionisia, Livia, Liviane, Leidiane, Luciene, and Liliane."

For Raimunda, Lindionésia is a synthesis and a desire. After tra-versing a life of war, João and Raimunda inscribed peace within the letters of their daughter's name. Their saga, however, has not yet come to a close in the hard reality of their days. In João and Raimunda's life, *peace* remains a word rather than the thing it represents.

There's something else to the *L*.

"It's for liberty. Liberty to express yourself, right? I wanted my daughters to be free, to have freedom of expression to study, play, be whatever they wanted in life."

Raimunda suspected peace might be closer the day João showed up and announced: "They're hiring at Tucuruí."

It was during this chapter that Raimunda discovered, as she puts it, that she had "sweet blood for dams." João's situation as a dam builder had forced him into a maze. If he had gone from dam to dam before, from project to project, now he had a family. João couldn't live on the *trecho* anymore. He needed to put down roots. As one of the dictatorship's most destructive dam projects came to life on the Tocantins River, again through João's hands, the couple landed and made their home. In the end, they discovered what happens when waters are held back: the forest is flooded and a piece of the Amazon dies. Raimunda recounts the moment when the circle closed in on João and he had his insight.

"My João started working on Tucuruí in 1976. In 1983, he real-ized he was like a pigeon. Because a pigeon builds her nest and then the day she lays her egg, she starts dismantling it. The day she fin-ishes taking the very last smidgen of the nest apart, her offspring has up and gone. And that's just what he was doing. Because he worked, and bought some land and a house with the money from the dam he was building. And that very dam flooded everything we had."

The Tucuruí hydroelectric power complex was a project of the dictatorship. And there was no negotiating with the dictatorship.

"We were, I'm not going to say stupid, but we were misinformed. What happened? The company said this: 'I can't deposit any money without the title on the property.' We had the title. But we never saw it again. And we couldn't prove anything, because it was their word against ours. So besides losing everything, we were made out to be liars in front of the judge who was there. This is why justice revolts me. There was never anything we could do. We couldn't afford a lawyer, we couldn't afford anything. They gave us some other land, where nobody could stand the mosquitoes or pests. The water rose because of the dam and rotted all the plant life. A sea of insects formed. There was no way to survive there. So what did we do? We took our young kids and went to Marabá, on the edge of the Trans-Amazonian Highway, at the very end of 1985. That didn't work out. In 1988 we came to the city of Altamira."

Along the Xingu River, João and Raimunda discovered there was a place where the poor could grow rich: the forest. But that came a bit later.

First, João endured two other trials. Not long after Tucuruí, he left for Iraq, hired by the Mendes Júnior Internacional construction company. Feeling like the victim of an undeclared war, João was deployed to the other side of the world to build "a roadway for war tanks." He suffered for a year, far from his family. He wanted to come back halfway through, but he'd signed a contract. From Iraq, he dictated a letter to Raimunda through his friend Francenildo, who knew how to write. He closed with these words: "Only love builds." The letter has been laminated, as proof that their love builds ties between banishments.

When he returned from the Middle East, João migrated around

"the Brazilian country" in search of work. He tells the following story to explain why he isn't able to beg, even though he hasn't had any way to earn his daily bread since he was kicked off the island:

"I've never asked for anything. I'd be ashamed to. I don't have it in me. I have it in me to starve to death, but I'm not brave enough to beg. Understand? Once I went to a company in Imperatriz, in Maranhão. I had twenty bucks. I hadn't eaten in three days. I wasn't eating because the money was for transportation. One night I'm on a bench in the bus station there, and one fellow says to the other, 'Buddy, over there in the town of Balsas they're hiring three and four at a time.' I got up and bought a ticket with my twenty bucks. I had two left. I got there, it was five a.m. I went over to the office and there was a sign out front: 'I'm not hiring anyone. And don't keep asking.' But just to be sure, I had a little breakfast back at the bus station, that left a buck and a half, and I went to chase down some work. When I'd stop by a restaurant, where people were eating, I'd ask for a glass of water and drink it. When it got to be noon, I went back and said to the guy, 'Buddy, there's no work and I don't have any money at all. I'm done for.' He said, 'Look, leave your bag here. Can you do stevedore work?' I said, 'I can do any kind of work.' He had a pile with eight hundred bags of fertilizer to unload at a nearby ranch. So then what happens? Before I'm halfway through the load, I couldn't take it anymore. There was this bottle of water there, and I drank the water and things started fading away, until I keeled over. I told them it had been four days since I'd eaten. When they finished putting the fertilizer away, the table was set, ready for people to have dinner. I wish you could've seen it, a complete spread! I put a couple spoons of rice and a little piece of meat on my plate. Mixed it up, ate half. Then I went off to drink a glass of water. And I threw it all back up. I got a shot at the drugstore—those shots that fortify you. But I didn't beg. Because I don't know how."

After João had passed first through the world and then through hunger, he rediscovered the river, this time not to interrupt it, but to be carried off by it. When he became a fisherman, João felt as if something had come to a close. Now he navigated.

The Turning Point
João and Raimunda Find Themselves Rich

The turn of the millennium marked João and Raimunda's discovery of the forest, not as something against or outside them, but as part of them. After journeying through what has been called progress and encountering nothing but trials, João and Raimunda were welcomed by one of the hundreds of islands in the Xingu. They learned how to harvest food from the forest, plant without harming the land, fish, and navigate. They took up the life of the fishermen and forest harvesters who have dual homes: one "outside" and one on the island or along the river.

"Outside" is how the people who live in the forest refer to the city, which in itself says much about their worldview. Their home "outside" is where they sell their goods at market, where they grapple with endless bureaucratic red tape, where they seek treatment for more complicated illnesses, and where their children study. Their home on the island or along the riverside is where they earn their living and live free. For the first time ever, João and Raimunda felt they had arrived. They had a place and not a single need. Hunger was a past tense.

They set their stakes deep. This was their life:

"We had our house on the island, where we got fish, beans, corn, pineapple, banana, golden spoon, green onions, parsley, chicory. All those were sources of income. I made money off all of them. I got the better part of it from the river. I'd come into the city with the things I'd planted, and my fish, and I made a lot of money in one week, cash in hand. I spent more time 'outside,' because I started getting involved in social movements. My husband lived there on the island. When he brought the fish in on Saturday, I'd sell it at market and go back with him. And I'd come back from there on Wednesday, on the water bus. I'd stay here waiting for him to bring fish again. That was our routine. During the holidays, at the end of the year, I'd stay there with him. Our life was back and forth. When you live on the river, you understand the river just like it understands you. You respect its limits and then it respects yours. It's a partnership between you and the waters. It's like this: The oar is my pen and the river, my slate."

João and Raimunda began by buying a stilt house in the lowlands of Altamira. Later, they built a brick home.

"It was a longtime dream to have a house on solid ground, on the land. The river gave us one. I was able to buy my refrigerator, my television, my gas stove, my gas tank. I was able to buy my bed, my mattress just like I wanted it. I went to the store and bought things, because I knew the river would pay me back. I'd be able to keep up the payments. The river was my bank, my credit card, my supermarket, my pharmacy, my store. I got everything from the river. Everything I have today came from within the Xingu. What the river didn't give us, the land did."

Raimunda immersed herself in the struggles of the Amazon. The women's struggle, the struggle for land, the struggle to save the environment. She joined the Workers' Party (Partido dos Trabalhadores, or PT) and became a human rights activist. Now she belonged. Her verb was no longer one of movement but of permanence. When Luiz Inácio Lula da Silva took office the first time, in 2003, the people in the social movements from Altamira and the region believed the Belo Monte Dam complex would be buried once and for all.

Ever since the 1970s, under the civil-military dictatorship, the Xingu power plant had been a threat that resurfaced with each new administration, even after Brazil had returned to democracy. In the past, the government-owned power utility Eletronorte called it "Kararaô," a war cry in the language of the Kayapo. A historic scene played out in 1989: an indigenous woman named Tuíra held a machete to the cheek of José Antônio Muniz Lopes, a director at Eletronorte. Tuíra's gesture expressed resistance to the damming of a river considered mythic by indigenous peoples. The photograph traveled the world. The power utility backtracked and changed the name of the plant to Belo Monte, "beautiful mountain."

No government had managed to get Belo Monte off the drawing board. Then Lula took office, with the electoral backing of the majority of the leaders and activists from social movements in the Amazon. He was a worker, "a sufferer, a man of the people who knew people's pain." Raimunda woke up feeling different. Her father had always been cautious about peace. He used to say it was a maybe. With Lula in power, Raimunda believed peace had acquired the consistency of a certainty.

At this point, and not any other, Sofia entered Raimunda's story and became her closest companion. "She's black, with kinky hair," as Raimunda describes her. Sofia is the first doll in her life. Raimunda was at a women's meeting in Belem, the capital of Pará, when she spotted a man selling dolls on the street for two dollars apiece. Raimunda thought the price was high, but she'd already fallen in love with one of the dolls. She took its name from a story that a nun had told her about a German woman named Sofia. The woman had been poor as a child, and when she grew up, she founded an institution to care for poor children. Now Sofia cares for Raimunda. She accompanies her all over the place, to a March of Daisies by women rural workers and to the United Nations Conference on Sustainable Development. Sofia travels hidden, because João guarantees "they'll poke fun at" Raimunda if they find out she carries a doll around in her purse. Raimunda, a grandmother of fifteen. "What Sofia means to me is a deep peace that has no answer," Raimunda says in her poetic prose.

It is only when she finds herself a place that Raimunda can have a doll.

"I wasn't ever a kid, because I had to work very hard. I wasn't ever a teenager either. That's why I won't give up my old age. I won't budge for anyone. My daughters say I'm losing my mind. No way. What I'm doing is living."

It would be years before Raimunda and so many other Amazon activists understood that they were facing yet another clash between different Brazils. Lula was a union leader from the ABC manufacturing region of São Paulo and his worldview was one of industry, concrete, the big city. For a manual laborer, progress was owning a car and flat-screen TV and enjoying barbecue and beer on the weekends. For a country, progress was transforming the Amazon into soybean fields and pastureland for cattle, while big mining companies shipped ore off for export. Lula wasn't familiar with this other type of living, the life of the forest. Nor did he think he had to be. Climate change was no big threat in his universe. His project for the Amazon has always resembled the dictatorship's, deeming the region a matter of national security, an unpeopled desert and a place ripe for exploitation. In the first decade of this century, commodity exports, especially to a booming China, were vital to funding antipoverty programs, boosting the real value of the minimum wage, and ensuring that some forty million Brazilians climbed the socioeconomic ladder, all without touching the privileges of the wealthiest. The agribusiness and mining sectors put increased pressure on the forest and indigenous lands while energy-intensive industries demanded more electric power. Chief among the major hydroelectric dams planned for the Amazon, Belo Monte became one of the biggest projects in Brazil's Growth Acceleration Program. On the Workers' Party's development agenda, nature paid the price, and it was steep.

Marina Silva's was the only voice in the federal government or the Workers' Party that had any strength to oppose the view that the Amazon was stuck back in the twentieth century. An environmental activist of international renown, she was raised in the rubber groves of Acre and was the mentee of leader Chico Mendes, murdered in 1988 for his role in the fight to save the Amazon forest. Marina could only stand the pressure until 2008, when she left the Ministry of the Environment and, shortly thereafter, the Workers' Party. Dilma Rousseff, Lula's chosen successor, never disguised her admiration for big Amazon projects or her unwillingness to listen to the peoples of the forest. Belo Monte started to materialize when she was Lula's minister of mines and energy.

Raimunda and the leading Xingu activists realized too late that only Lula could get Belo Monte off the drawing board, precisely because he was Lula. On the one hand, the Workers' Party in power disarmed Brazil's social movements; on the other, it coopted them. Regional parliamentarians who had previously proclaimed speech after speech against the power plant switched to defending "development." Resistance to Belo Monte had been unified for decades, but now it split. The electric power industry had sailed through various administrations as a fiefdom of José Sarney, oligarch from Maranhão and former president. One example is José Antônio Muniz Lopes, the man who felt the indigenous woman Tuíra's machete against his cheek in 1989. He spent the entire string of administrations under Brazil's democratic rule holding posts in various government-owned power utilities. And he still does. "Only the collar changed, the dog's the same," says Raimunda, explaining that the reins of the country's profitable power industry do not change hands. But only the Workers' Party and Lula had enough political might to undermine the resistance and make Belo Monte a concrete reality in the middle of the Xingu.

The endeavor to erect an engineering project expected to cost over $14 billion is underpinned by an alliance not only of groups that have been on the scene for a long while, like the Brazilian Democratic Movement Party (PMDB), but also of some newer arrivals, like the Workers' Party. Construction companies form the third element—or the first, depending on the observer's vantage point. These interests, woven through decades of administrations, also explain why Belo Monte is becoming a fait accompli, despite the facts that the Federal Prosecutor Office has filed twenty-three lawsuits alleging that the project violates the constitution, President Dilma Rousseff's administration is in tatters, and a number of top construction firm owners are serving time for corruption. Belo Monte may be the knot that when untangled reveals Brazil.

As far as Raimunda was concerned, there was only one conclusion to be reached. For her, as for so many others, the Workers' Party was never meant to be just another party in power but rather a political project entwined with her search for a place in Brazil and with the belief that this place exists. She took this symbolism literally. When she felt she'd been betrayed, she lost faith in democracy.

"If Lula would look at the people who elected him, he'd never build Belo Monte. It's hard for me to say this, but I voted for Lula and I voted for Dilma. And they betrayed us. Because Lula plainly said Belo Monte wasn't going to happen, and then Dilma said Belo Monte was necessary. They're traitors of humanity. Oh, good Lord! If I saw them, I wouldn't say a thing. I'd go straight for their throats, so they'd learn to have shame. What kind of president lies to a nation? I'm not ever going to vote again. If I didn't need my voter ID, I'd rip it up. What I plan to do is not put my ballot in the box anymore. I don't know if it's right, but that's my plan."

As Raimunda sees it, Belo Monte is the "monster" that reveals the contradictions of the party she once believed to be hers. Not the party seen as having betrayed the middle class when it displayed the stain of corruption, but the party Raimunda feels has reneged on its very reason for being: to defend the weak and the unprotected; those who have historically been torn off their land, including indigenous peoples; and those who have historically been exiled within their own country, such as Raimunda herself. It is at this place on the map, at the final frontier for someone who has roamed Brazil in search of peace, that the Workers' Party's stance about defending the poor has rung false for a long time. But since the Amazon is a far-flung elsewhere for Brazil's economic and political center, these voices have been ignored.

Raimunda wants the floor.

"I'll say something else: The river is sick and the fish are all doped up, woozy from the lack of oxygen. Nobody has any idea how big this monster on the Xingu is. Nobody knows what's going to happen when it starts up. Nobody."

The only thing missing for Belo Monte to come onstream is its operating license. Raimunda and all those who belong to the river fear this like someone who expects to hear the world will end before Christmas.

The Interruption
"Belo Monster" Blocks Raimunda and João's Life

After João's legs and voice locked up at the Norte Energia office, he has never again been the same man who made his way through diverse Brazils and diverse hungers. In May 2015, Raimunda took him to Belem to look for treatment. They were to return only three months later. Meanwhile, their daughters saw to moving out of the house in Altamira. They knew their mother wouldn't have stood for it had she been in town, ready instead to hold out for a fair value. When Raimunda and João got back, they didn't have a home "outside" anymore. In exchange, they were paid $24,000, not enough to buy a house of similar size, quality, and location.

Raimunda recycled 3,500 bricks from her neighbors' demolished homes to start building hers in a housing project outside the city. The couple's canoe became a displaced object, resting on dry land miles from the river. Raimunda plans to use it to make a bench for visitors when their house is ready.

Two of the three dogs that lived with João and Raimunda on the island couldn't bear life on a leash in the city and passed away. The first to die was Barão do Triunfo, Baron of Victory, a large Brazilian mastiff mixed breed who kept watch over their house from the bow of the canoe. "I gave him that name because he was a lord," Raimunda explains. Xena, a pit bull so christened because she was "as authoritarian as the princess" of film and cartoon fame, was the second to be found dead. "I couldn't let them run loose outdoors because they get violent in the city. But I didn't know they'd die. If I'd known, I would've let them die loose, so they'd die free. They died on the leash," a guilt-ridden Raimunda laments. "Myself, I don't know if I'll ever be free of this leash that Norte Energia put on me. I keep rambling around, getting lost, going to a home that isn't there anymore." The only dog left is the mongrel Negão, Big Blackie, "a dog that doesn't get excited so easy." Named neither after a princess nor after a baron, Negão endures, like his owner, Raimunda.

In order to have "proof," Raimunda documented her forced exodus in photographs and on video. She divides it into before, during, and after Belo Monte. In the "during" phase, two of her daughters went to work on the hydroelectric project, one in the kitchen, the other at the mechanics shop. Raimunda fought with them. "This is just like winnings from gambling. You can't do this to me," she raged. "It took a while, but I freed my daughters." Pink camera in hand, she even captured the National Public Security Force protecting Belo Monte from the people. "Just look, they think I'm the threat."

Raimunda recounts her journey as she flips through the images on an out-of-date cell phone.

Life before Belo Monte: "I documented my whole history waiting for the future, and the future's here. Before Belo Monte, this was my story. Look, my house. My garden, my little orchard, all neat and tidy. All swept clean, just right. Here's my old man with his fields, clearing the land. This here is lemongrass for medicine, for diarrhea, things like that. Here's golden spoon, hanging heavy, in a later stage. Look at this golden spoon! They burned it. Everything's been burned. Here, some friends visiting me. Manioc, looking nice and pretty. Look here, my dog Negão. For them, this wasn't anything; for me it was everything. Here's the friend I was talking about, this one, my Buddha belly plant. I'd get home and that was the first I saw. My Buddha belly. Look at the riverbank. Look here. My other dog, who died of sorrow because he wasn't used to a leash, and I tied him up. We'll stop here."

Life during Belo Monte: "Now I'm going to show you during Belo Monte. During the process of back-and-forth, back-and-forth, back-and-forth. Here's my boat. Right here. Here's my gas stove, my wood stove . . . living off the river is so enjoyable. If you know what it's all about. If you don't, you don't appreciate it. My husband planting . . . look here. Planting manioc, because the rains were coming, so he was getting ready. My dog, that I don't have anymore . . . the other dog, he died too. My old man. We've shared our lives for thirty-eight years, always together. I cut, he plants. Today he's sitting in a chair, waiting for our house to get done. Here's the weekend I fenced it in, because of the chickens, so I could plant some green onions. But it didn't work because the chickens were faster than me. This here's my old blue-eyed white man, a dreamboat. Today he's . . . I tell him he's not worthless because I can still see him in front of me. So he's still my dreamboat. And there's another angle of the island, here, where it's productive. Let me show you here . . . the plants that were burned. The ones that were closer to the house, they burned those, wiped them all out. This is in the winter. See, we plant and harvest during the high waters, because they come but always on a certain date. Look at my vegetable garden: green onions, parsley . . . me picking tomatoes, ginger. That's for headaches, diarrhea, bloating. Home remedies. And here's me, in the water, I love the water. Here's me afraid of a snake. It got ahead of me and I went after it. But it was faster than me, it got away. We sleep in the hammock in the winter. My grandson, who came to spend some vacation with me. My lemongrass plant. It doesn't die in the water either, see, it stays underwater a bit. It only dies if these leaves get covered up. But if it can breathe, it doesn't die. My house, the one Norte Energia didn't think was a house. A banana tree . . . just look, loaded with bunches of bananas. Manioc nice and tall. Look at the corn here. Loaded with corn. Here's me afraid of the snake again. It's afraid of me, I'm afraid of it. So, this here . . . it's the end of the story of the life of an island, which is very important to me. Because I didn't live on the island. I lived from it, and it lived from me. Because we were like friends. Pineapple. More corn. Look at the corn back there. Look at the size of this bunch of bananas. Let me show you here. This here, look, it's not just fruit to eat, it's an insect antidote. There's fishermen who live on the island, and I lived from the island. I nurtured it, and it nurtured me. We were friends. Understand? Let me show you a picture here where the river goes away, says goodbye."

Life after Belo Monte: "Here I was, wondering: When will this day come? When I don't want to leave. My son-in-law saying too late, nothing more to be done about it, that's that. And me telling him I still had hope. Here's me telling my plants I was going but I'd be back. But it was a lie, I didn't come back. My old man wondering if he'd be back someday or not: 'Do you suppose I'll ever come back here?' I told him, 'I don't know. God does.' Look at me here staring at the horizon, asking God to let us stay on the island. My husband crying. This here's all burned. Norte Energia burned it. Look at this. All that beauty I showed you, that golden spoon, such a beautiful thing. Here it is, scorched. I went there, recorded it again. I recorded the before, the during, and the after of Belo Monte. Look here. Nothing's left. They say there's always evidence of a crime left behind. They left it. Look here. Impunity only exists because justice doesn't speak up. As long as justice has that blindfold on—that statue they made there in Brasilia, she looks like this. Justice only sees who she wants to. When she doesn't want to see someone, she doesn't."

Raimunda wants to write a book. She already has the title: *A Fisherman's Story: Before, During, and After Belo Monte*. She's beginning to think her only place will be her grave. She's already ordered her shroud, "out of satin, white for peace."

ACT 3

The Impasse

In drawing the layout for her new house, Raimunda made sure it wasn't at all like the one that was destroyed. "I don't want a door where you go in through the front anymore, I want a door where you go in through the side, because I want my future to be different, so I started with my home's infrastructure," she explains. "When I go into this house now, I don't want to think I'm in the other one." Raimunda has traced out her path through the new house, still under construction. The walls are green "because that's hope in the future," the baseboards are brown to show "the barrier of the dam," the window gratings are black "as a sign of mourning."

"There's a story to everything in my life," she says. And there is.

Raimunda is a maker of meanings and she goes through life

stitching them one to the other. João does not. The day he became paralyzed, he lost his ability to find meaning. Inside himself, he stays locked up. He's like a man who looked at the sun: the brilliance blinded him. He doesn't know how to get back, or what his destination is, since there is nowhere there. "I lost the end of the thread. I'm inside this house today, but truth is, all the time, I don't have a house. Understand? I'm outside. I get lost. I don't know where I am. I've lost my way from everything." He fumes, his eyes like a river during an Amazon storm. "I'm worse than Dilma, because she lost the country's way, but I lost my way home."

That's the impasse between João and Raimunda today.

Raimunda says:

"I'm a *pindoba* palm, a plant everyone in Maranhão goes after. The more Belo Monte rips bark off me, the more I revive. I was burned up inside, like my island, but I revive. The *pindoba* is like that, nobody can kill it off with fire or by yanking it up. It comes back. Like me. I come from people who have suffered a lot by nature. Suffering is part of our history. I'm not going to die just because I took a beating. No way. I'm descended from slaves and from an indigenous ethnic group that's almost extinct. I come from people who suffered way back. I'm a *pindoba* and I want to live."

João replies, and it's as if the two of them are engaged in a poetic dialogue:

"But I'm not like that. When I lost the island, I lost my life. I lost my way. It stopped there, understand? From here on in, I only see darkness in my sight. I don't see a clear world anymore. I see nothing but darkness. I stay here staring at the world, looking for myself. Who can answer this search for me? Nobody. The hole in my life, the hole in my life . . ."

The impasse came to a head on September 4, 2015. That day, João "went crazy" at home. Raimunda tells what happened:

"João called the family to go out to the burned island. To serve

as a martyr. He wants to kill himself there, in protest. I said I wasn't
going and wouldn't let him either. If he kills himself out there on
the island, I warned him that I'll leave him there to be eaten by the
vultures. That's why I took his canoe away. He can get anywhere on
the river, rowing or swimming. But he gets lost outside."

João closes his brutal poem:

"I want the world to know that Belo Monte killed me."

CAPTIVITY

The Sapucaia do Sul Zoo once housed a monkey named Alemão (Kraut). One bright Sunday, Alemão managed to open the lock and escape. He had the world's broad horizon waiting for him. He had the trees in the forest within reach of his fingers. He had the wind whispering promises in his ears. Alemão had all of this. He'd spent his life trying to open that lock. But when he succeeded, he turned his back on it all. Instead of taking the plunge into freedom, unknown and unguaranteed, Alemão walked over to the restaurant, packed with visitors. He grabbed a beer and sat there at the counter downing it. The humans fled in fright.

Why did they flee?

The monkey had turned into a man.

The disturbing thing about this true story is not the resemblance between man and monkey. All this is as old as Darwin. The horrifying thing is that, like humans, the monkey turned his back on freedom. And went to the bar for a cold one.

A zoo has many purposes, some of them edifying. But a zoo serves primarily to give humans, as they stand in front of someone else's cage, the chance to make certain of their own freedom, and their superiority as a species. Then they can return to their apartment with its fifteen-year mortgage, satisfied with their lives; open their security door with its metal bars, contented with their key chain; and lodge themselves on the couch in front of the TV. Wake up Monday morning happy to punch the time clock, happy to be human, and free.

There are two ways to visit a zoo: with or without innocence. The former is easier, and the only way with satisfaction guaranteed. The latter might prove a gloomy journey into a mirror, with no glamour and no going back.

Come along, if you'd like.

The sacred baboon has an ordinary Brazilian name: Beto. The most dangerous kind of fury, that of impotence, lies lurking where his eyes merge with his mind. Beto moves round and round the cage, pummeling the bars. He throws food and feces at the visitors. He beats his mate if she doesn't do everything he wants. She isn't allowed to utter a sound without his permission or budge without his acquiescence. If she does, Beto cuffs her roundly. If they separate her from him, Beto gets worse. He starts tearing off pieces of his own body. During these fits, Beto takes ten milligrams of Valium a day.

The Bengal tigers are kings in disguise. They have voices, they have muscles; they are magnificent. But when they're born into captivity, they enter the world stripped of their essence. They are a wish that will never come true. They divine Asia's humid jungles but can't even recognize the stars. When the sun slips over the metropolitan region, they're locked up in stone caverns, claustrophobic. Prey is pointless for a hunter who eats horse meat from a slaughterhouse. Rage is pointless for someone who sleeps curled up, exiled not from what he was but from what he might have been, and will never be.

Years ago, one of their great-grandfathers scaled his keeper's ladder and peered beyond the walls. That's the farthest any of them got. They're powerful, these Bengal tigers. But when the time comes for them to be confined to the dark cave of their slavery, they turn their backs to the moon that rises like a promise and march into their cage, downtrodden, submissive, the sorriest beasts in the forest.

The Andean bear is named Fuzzy, as if she were a stuffed animal. Her son is called Rayban, and he's just as cute. When Rayban was born, Fuzzy did what mothers usually do: taught him the art of resignation. She dragged him by his ear over to the bowels of the cavern at the scheduled time. Now Rayban goes of his own volition. But every day Rayban defies his mother, stretching up to test the lock. Never having breathed the frigid fragrance of his ancestors' mountain range, Rayban can't guess what's on the other side. But he intuits it. And because he's a cub, he still hasn't abandoned his pursuit.

Pinky lives alone. The other two elephants, Nellie and Mohan, fell into the pit and perished. The pit is the elephants' prison. Mohan spent six years chained up, because his species' place of captivity wasn't ready yet. When they released him, he lasted three months. He died trying to reach freedom . . . or perhaps just one of the dogs that wander about the zoo and are found torn to pieces. Of the three, Nellie was always the most untamable. Nineteen years ago, she killed a visitor, a man from Criciúma, Minas Gerais, who was celebrating his retirement. Newly freed from the dismal solitude of the coal mines where he had worked, he mounted Nellie. She knocked him to the ground and crushed his head. So alike in their tragedies, elephant and man.

There were three occasions when Nellie plunged into the pit. On one of those occasions, she lost part of her belly and a breast, but she didn't give up. She died the third time, trying. Since she never forgets, Pinky the elephant absorbed the example, and convinced herself that ruthless punishment awaits anyone who dares to take one step beyond what is permitted.

The insight gained from this subversive trip to the zoo is that animals grow human in captivity. Incarceration snatches life, desire, and pursuit from them. More and more they come to resemble the people who seek them out, certain they'll find an alibi there. The questions are dangerous:

What would happen if you found the key to your life's invisible lock? What if you vaulted the pit of your daily routine? What if you took the elephant's step?

Maybe it would be easier to walk over to the counter and have a cold one.

THE WOMAN WHO NOURISHED

"It's so strange," she says. "I spent my whole life punching a time clock, everything on a schedule. When I retired, I ripped off my watch and threw it out. I thought I'd finally be free. Then this disease came along. When I finally had time, I discovered my time was up."

This betrayal by life intrigues her. When she talks, her expression is one of perplexity. Ailce de Oliveira Souza isn't a philosopher; she's a retired *merendeira*, a school lunch lady. Her whole life has been utterly concrete, sometimes brutally so. Her whole life has been a sequence of acts. And now death has come along demanding metaphors.

It's sunny outside and her neighbors are living out the first part of Manuel Bandeira's poem. "When the funeral passed by, the men who were in the café took off their hats mechanically, paid their respects absentmindedly. All of them were turned toward life, absorbed in life, confident of life." Inside, seated in her living room, each on a sofa and facing the other, she and I are living out the second act. "Yet one doffed his hat in a slow and sweeping gesture, staring long at the coffin. This man knew that life is fierce agitation to no purpose, that life is betrayal."

Ailce has never gotten over the feeling that she was betrayed by "this disease," as she puts it most of the time, or "the tumor." She doesn't utter the word *cancer*. When we met, on March 26, 2008, it had been nearly a year since her skin had yellowed and she had been flooded by nausea. She's going through a period of great rage against God. The betrayal is his.

Ailce's cancer is a stone in the middle of the road—the road being her bile ducts. The tumor has blocked the passageway, and since the bile can't flow out, it is released into her bloodstream, leaving her yellow all over. When she acquired this sunlit color, Ailce wasn't yet sixty-six, and she thought she was enjoying the best time of her life. "No kids, no husband, no commitments, retired, free," she sums things up. She had planned to see the work of Aleijadinho in the historic towns of Minas Gerais and visit the Spain of Sarita Montiel's films. She has discovered that when she travels, she forgets everything else. And, no matter what her destination, when the landscape rushes by the bus window, she feels she's going where she has always wanted to. "Have you ever noticed how we change when we travel?"

Ailce used to take the bus everywhere, go to senior dances, and once got involved with a younger man. "I feel light when I dance, free, free, let loose," she says. "Can you believe that the more I dance, the more I want to?" She prefers dancing alone because it gives her the freedom to twirl around the floor without anyone leading her. She's always wanted to run her own life. So she chooses her steps on the dance floor, while inside her twirling body, her cells are silently betraying her.

If *cancer* is the word she doesn't say, *freedom* is the word she repeats. Here again, the concreteness of Ailce's life. She is tied up, literally; her life depends on two hoses jabbed inside her. They drain bile from her body, and discharge into two plastic containers that she carries around in a grocery bag when she moves about the house, or in a tote bag decorated with Disney princesses when she goes out. One day a security guard at a supermarket scowled at her bile bag. He thought she was shoplifting. Embarrassed to carry bodily fluids around in a sack, Ailce gradually quit going out. She turned the music off at home and doesn't dance anymore.

Being tied up horrifies her. She spent her whole life rebelling to escape a metaphorical prison, and now she's attached not to the invisible threads that have always bound her to the world's conventions but to two synthetic hoses that drain the polluted river out of her body. "I think we're worthless. Look what comes out of me."

Ailce didn't know what was going to happen. When she went into the operating room, she thought it was only for some complicated test. "The doctor was singing to calm me down. I don't remember the song. The anesthesia put me to sleep and when I came to, I was on a gurney out in the hall. I was shaking hard. I had the chills and was freezing cold. There was a blanket folded on top of me, and the nurse threw on another. But I couldn't get warm. So the doctor had them give me a shot, and it calmed me down. Then I saw the drains and realized I was tied up."

She soon learns that I'm a third thread in her life. She's never had a chance to talk much about herself. She enjoys this drainage of words. "We store things up our whole life. When I talk, it's like they're being released inside me. It frees me." On the other end of this thread, I too feel tied to her.

Ailce is an ordinary woman. She never thought her life could become a novel. Or even a news story. She didn't summit Mount Everest or decipher a DNA helix or compose a symphony. Nor did she burn her bra in the streets. Ailce lived.

As Ailce tells her story, she begins deciphering little singularities that used to pass her by unnoticed, in a life where time was devoured by shifts at work. Ailce realizes there's no way to lend meaning to death, but she can lend it to life. Only then can she tolerate the cold surface of an end she is already touching with her hands. To live so close to death, she has to divine the contexture of life. Otherwise, all she's left with are those synthetic hoses.

Ailce has always wanted to "free myself," but like many of us, she never really managed to define from what. Then she learned she would have to confront not medicine but poetry: "All of us who live have one life that is lived and another that is thought. And the only life we have is this one that is divided between the true and the false."

Intuitively, Ailce knows her sanity depends on confronting the chaos of life more than the chaos of death, which is merely an end point, generally an improvised one. And then, with effort and not without suffering, she can come to terms with all the loose ends, the interrupted patterns, the crooked seams in the weave of the life she has lived. The hardest thing for her to accept is that some stitches will be left undone. Or worse, they will be sewn without her.

The fourth of nine children, she is the second-to-the-last whose name starts with the letter A: Ailton, Amilton, Adailton, Ailce. Then come Adilson, Deusdete, Osvaldo, José Adnnann, and Berenice. "There were such a lot of us," she says. "I just wished I had more room, a place just my own." At the end of her life, she has not only a little corner but a house all her own. Spacious, two stories, the house is the concrete embodiment of her hard work. She sacrificed a great deal for her home. When she got sick, she discovered that the house had become a prison. All she wants now is to free herself from it. But every week, every month, her space shrinks. First, the front gate marks the boundary of her world. Then the front door. Next, her territory is confined to the second story. In the end, all she has is her bedroom.

Then Ailce shuts the window in the sun's face and doesn't leave her bed anymore. This is when she learns it is possible to live in your memory, and she reviews the itinerary of her life. She was

born in São Romão, a small town in Minas Gerais that grew out
of bloody sagas. Her childhood fit into a span between the largesse
of the São Francisco River and a stream called Escuro, which ran
alongside her family's farm. She grew up surrounded by water on
all sides, but was afraid of swimming. Her father was a boat cap-
tain, a police officer, and a justice of the peace. Her mother was a
strong woman, and in her second marriage. Wed at thirteen, she'd
fled her first marriage with a daughter named Maria in tow. She
kept her home and children tidy, always in shoes, with immacu-
lately white towels sewn and embroidered by her and the kitchen
engulfed in a fog of fragrant steam.

These olfactory memories, composed of spices, pork rind, and
sweetness cooked together in her mother's cast-iron pots, have stayed
with Ailce her whole life. Close to death, they grow more vivid.
When the toxins released by the tumor poison her body and everything makes her nauseous, Ailce recalls the black beans with pork,
the little cheese buns, and the cassava cookies, and her castigated
mouth is soothed by saliva from her childhood. Ailce, who can no
longer eat, feasts on reminiscences and relishes food made by her
mother, who died years ago. Forty pounds thinner, not enough
strength left to walk to the bathroom, she still longs for Dona Santa's
cornbread.

Ailce abandoned her parents' home at the age of eighteen. São
Romão had slowly shrunk in the face of her yearnings as a young
woman. It seemed as if the town, once so spacious, had sprouted
walls. "I was raised in a world where black people were black, the
poor were poor, farmers were farmers, and maids were maids," she
says. "I wanted to move on. I always wanted to discover new things."

She slipped on the map and landed in Guarulhos, in the state
of São Paulo, at an older brother's home, where she once again felt
confined. Ailce had altered her geography but not her destiny. For
her the 1960s were not crazy years. She was a laborer, a factory

seamstress. It was among thread, needles, and bobbins that she first heard revelations about sex, when a friend from work came back after her wedding night and said not only did it hurt, but at the end, a gooey white liquid squirted out of the man's organ. Ailce filed this information away so she wouldn't look surprised when her time came.

Around then, Ailce fell in love with a light-skinned, green-eyed fellow, and she, who had always been very practical, took up day-dreaming. Squeezed into a foldout cot she shared with another tenant in the kitchen, Ailce, who wasn't much of a smiler, talked of love and laughed for no reason. One Saturday she announced: "We're going to the dance tonight wearing new dresses." Then Ailce, proud of her twenty-one-inch waist, sewed a billowing skirt for each. Much later, she would forget the synthetic hoses that jabbed into her liver, as she remembered her blue organza frock. But the handsome young fellow didn't want anything to do with marriage, and Ailce locked up her heart.

Ever since those days, Ailce has never gone out without fixing herself up. "Ailce comes to her appointments looking very pretty, hair colored, earrings on, high heels, nicely dressed," wrote Dr. Maria Goretti Maciel in her chart at the palliative care unit of the Hospital do Servidor Público Estadual, a public health care facility in São Paulo, on April 2, 2008. Ailce has checked into the hospital on shaky legs but in high heels more than once. "I'm very finicky," she says to explain her theory that a woman should only go out in public looking impeccable. Ailce will die when she loses the heels upon which she has always balanced herself, even on life's down-grades. Maybe this is why, since she still cannot utter the word *death*, she uses the metaphor *fall*. "I'm not going to fall," she says. "I won't put up with falling."

At twenty-three, she made a pragmatic decision. She married a laborer named Jaime, a neighbor's brother, ten years her senior. He was the well-groomed type, who didn't set foot outside the house without brilliantine in his hair and polished shoes. "I didn't want to live at somebody else's place anymore, I wanted a place of my own," recalls Ailce. "He was honest, hardworking, wore a suit and tie, came from a good family. I got married."

Ailce couldn't know then that such a distinguished young man would have an inordinate urge to drink. Or that a substantial share of her future would be spent living the always sad—and always so cliché—fate of an alcoholic's wife. In Ailce's case, it was sadder still because there was none of the originality she had planned for herself. She signed the marriage certificate convinced romantic love was an illusion no longer appropriate to the adult world awaiting her. Perhaps this was Ailce's first capitulation, despite her dreams. By the time she got sick, her wedding ring had long since disappeared from her finger. "It doesn't fit anymore," she says. "It's tight."

Her husband was "of the Spanish race, hot-blooded." All this fire eventually incinerated Ailce, who already had her first child nestled in a curve of her belly when she got married. It was only much later that she learned there was a name for what she had felt when Marcos was born, by C-section. At first it was an intense love, as she counted every finger and toe, adding up to ten many times, just to make sure. Then she started crying alone, ashamed of her thoughts. "I didn't want that life. I wanted a different one," she says. "So I rejected it."

Many years later, when Sunday television shows began addressing women's issues, Ailce was relieved to discover she had suffered from postpartum depression, common among many women, and not an existential crisis in which she questioned what had happened to her great hopes. When those first weeks of motherhood turned into months, she went back to feeling such intense love for her son that now, near the end, she still believes no other woman takes care of him as well as she does.

When a second new life announced its presence inside her, Ailce cried again. Once more her husband had drunk too much and climbed into bed to lie with her. Ailce grabbed a blanket and curled up on the floor. She felt trapped in a web she hadn't planned to spin. Maybe that was why she was so afraid of spiders? "I cried and cried and cried. That wasn't the life I'd wanted for myself," she says. "Then I started to calm down. Maybe my baby would be a girl, and I really wanted a girl." Luciane was born tiny, allergic to milk, and with the strong personality typical of the women in the family. She was an odd little girl, who from the age of seven would hide in her mother's bed so she wouldn't be assailed by things from the other world.

These very different children give Ailce the two threads she uses to tie up the end of her life. Marcos, who got his undergraduate degree in education and like Ailce took a civil service exam for a public school job, cares for his mother's bodily wounds. At forty-two, he's a quiet man who keeps his emotions locked away somewhere between his heart and stomach and who rarely loses his cool. Upon entering a room, he occupies a corner. When his mother fell ill, he learned to change her bandages, empty bags and clean drains, dispense her meds, and make her breakfast.

As she grows weaker, Marcos starts bathing her. "Don't be embarrassed by your mother, son," says Ailce. "Your mother gave you lots of baths." It is this silent son, with his courage to confront his mother's flesh, who transforms the horror of the disease into everyday tenderness. Through his touch, he enables Ailce to tolerate a body whose bile flows on the outside.

When she likens her body to an infant's to vanquish the mother-son taboo, Ailce signals the loss of what is female in her. "The disease has taken everything from me. I've lost my breasts, butt, waistline, everything," she says. "Nothing's left." Ailce thus concerns herself less and less with the nakedness of a body that betrays her in every way and seems to belong only to the disease.

Luciane's tiny figure is always in the center. She fills in the silence with words and, like her mother, finds meaning in action. Once she had grown up, she came to terms with the supernatural by becoming a *mãe de santo*, a priestess in the Afro-Brazilian religion known as Candomblé. Luciane scoured her family's history and discovered that her maternal grandmother was a gypsy. In Rio de Janeiro, where she lives with her husband, she throws a yearly party in honor of an ancestor named Carmen, who speaks Spanish through Luciane's mouth. Ailce accepts the mystery, and although she's never learned the language, she chats with Carmen like an old friend.

Luciane lends her mother's life a mystical dimension. Through this daughter, Ailce finds meanings for a way of being in a world that has always been so concrete for her. Luciane gives her mother a history that extends beyond her own, and gives her a place in this history. Near the end, Ailce's small life gains meaning within a larger tapestry. Every November, Ailce is the one who lights the fire of ancestry, donning colorful skirts, her figure cloaked in a solemnity that resists the plainness of a life of time cards. Then she twirls about to the sound of a gypsy violin and at last, her feet in the air, not even brushing the ground, she touches a freedom she had only sensed before. Because she has a past before her birth, she will have a future after her death.

From my sometimes uncomfortable place as observer of a family portrait, now inside the scene, now outside, I ask myself if these children, each in their own way, understand the magnitude of what they give their mother. The two of them are not irreconcilable, as they sometimes believe, but complementary. Ailce needs what each one can give her, to the end.

Ailce discovered her tumor only when she was sent to the palliative care unit, after seven months of treatment at another department of the hospital. She suspected the diagnosis, but preferred not to know for sure. In palliative care, the truth corners her. "Before, the doctors spoke in that language of theirs, scientific words, and I didn't understand. Once in a while, I'd hear the word *tumor*. But I never asked," she says. "They told me in palliative care. I started asking: 'Listen, doctor, is what I have serious?' The doctors said it was a tumor. I asked if it was malignant, they said yes. 'But can't you operate?' Then they did a drawing. They showed me how it was a tumor in a spot where it couldn't be messed with. I thought, well, it can't be removed, but I'll have chemo and get better. But then the oncologist said I couldn't have chemo. So it started dawning on me. I got terribly upset. I thought God didn't exist. Me, who always wanted to go farther, couldn't go anywhere anymore."

Ailce tells the story—and immediately "forgets" the diagnosis. During subsequent visits, she tests me: "I don't think there's anything in me anymore." Ailce has much hope that I'll confirm her magical thinking. At these moments, my throat aches from the words I can't utter but would very much like to say.

Unable to cope with my silence, she hedges. "It's a good thing I don't have any pain. I couldn't handle pain." Lourdes, hired to clean house, cook, and care for Ailce, comes to her rescue: "You don't have cancer. I had an aunt with cancer and she screamed from pain. And she smelled bad. The smell was so awful nobody got close to her. You don't smell at all. I change your sheets and clothes and they don't smell at all. As far as I'm concerned, you don't have anything." Two women alone in that house, and one of them has a death sentence. They watch me from the corners of their eyes, wary that I'll destroy the fragile balance of their miracle with my words.

It's early April, and Ailce is happy because her appetite is back. It's a result of the palliative care, which eases the nausea and overall symptoms. "I ate seconds at lunch," she announces. Ailce pampers her orchids, talks with her plants, dirties her hands in the soil, shows up at family parties. She gets the urge to buy new clothes and take a bus across town. She longs for prosaic activities that now are rich as rarities: taking a shower, the water cascading over her, without worries that she'll harm the holes for her drains; sleeping on her stomach, which she can't do anymore. Ailce is living out sunshiny days. She's eating, she's cured.

I need to eat, too. She won't let me leave her house without a second helping of cake, cheese buns, cookies. This is a ritual that I, raised in the countryside, can understand. Only later do I realize that, for Ailce, offering food is the key to a life. She became a school lunch lady after passing a civil service exam with a score of 9.5 out of 10. For twenty-seven years, she fed poor children. On Monday mornings, she would welcome them with a mug of milk so they would have the strength to enter the classroom. It was her mission to keep them alive. It was she who worked the miracle of getting children faint with hunger to run about the playground.

Ailce loved this power. Her father wanted to pay for her schooling as a teacher, but she wasn't interested. She wanted to become a nurse, but couldn't. Filling the bellies of famished children lent greatness to her life. "I never got there late. I'd work when I was sick because I knew they needed me. They were very poor kids, you know? Gosh, those kids gobbled down their food. I'd make soup, chocolate milk, pudding. It was real tasty. Sometimes I'd make six ten-gallon pots. And they'd eat it all up. Every little bit. On Mondays there'd be so many kids who would pass out, get sick. Because they'd go Saturday and Sunday without any nourishment. On Mondays they'd show up pale, white-lipped, you know? That's how it was. They'd gobble it all up, poor little things. I think that was all they had to eat. I couldn't do anything outside of school, but there they ate their fill."

Before Ailce was sent to palliative care, a doctor who lacked the courage to tell her the truth said: "You need to eat a lot to put on weight. Then, when you're stronger and have more energy, we can operate." He doesn't know what effect this had on her. Eat, get strong, and get better has been the mantra of Ailce's life. It's everything that makes sense to her.

Weeks before she dies, her nails are still dug into this hope. The palliative care doctors have assured her the tumor can't be removed, but she is still locked into the only chance for staying alive that they gave her. Between one doctor, who suggested a cure was possible, and all the others, who have only the truth to give, it's obvious she'd rather believe the former. Therefore, getting better is her responsibility now. But she, who always filled everyone else's belly, is unable to fill her own because of her nausea. And because she is unable to eat, she's not strong enough for surgery. Without surgery, there is no cure. Her requiem reaches its most dramatic notes: not only will Ailce die, it'll be her own fault.

In mid-May, Ailce gets worse. The nausea returns full force, and food won't go down her throat. The palliative home-care team is ever more diligent. They unclog her drains, change dressings, do what is possible to keep Ailce from spending her days in a hospital bed. Her medications are switched at outpatient appointments, but she has reached a critical phase of the disease. She is consumed by despair because she can't nourish herself. She asks the doctors for medicine "to perk up my appetite." But no food is prepared the way she has instructed, and every seasoning turns bitter in her mouth. Ailce blames the woman who has taken her place in the kitchen for not doing for her what she spent her life doing for children faint from hunger. In the intimacy of her home, it is a time of high drama for both women. Ailce reaches the unbearable: she, who always nourished everyone else, will die because she is unable to eat.

Ailce stands four foot seven, but fights as if she were the size of a female volleyball player. By June it is hard for her to bring a glass to her lips without spilling water or put one leg in front of the other to walk. But she does all this. Shaking, filled with rage. "Get your hand off my arm, I can walk by myself," she says. "But you'll fall," her worried daughter responds. "I won't," she shoots back. Her daughter tries to give her some café au lait. She grits her teeth. "I've got to drink it myself." She spills the coffee, but she's the one who holds the cup in both hands. I ask Ailce why it's so important to hold the cup. "I've got to be myself, understand?" I realize then that she will die when she can no longer hold the cup. She will die when the last trace of autonomy slips through her yellow hands and shatters on the floor.

Around this time, Ailce is at the edge of the impossible: she's "forgotten" the disease, but the disease hasn't forgotten her. She blames the doctors because she sees no "progress." On at least two occasions, the family considers consulting other providers, different hospitals. Then they change their minds. They're afraid of what they'll hear at the close of the appointment. They'd rather not dynamite this remaining room for doubt.

Then the storm hits. On the morning of June 19, after a night of jarring dreams, Ailce announces she wants to die. It doesn't seem to me like she does. What she's saying, but inside out, is that she wants to live. In her feisty way, she's asking for help. An hour later I find her in the hospital cafeteria, eyes afloat in tears, hands trembling, sitting with two unfamiliar women who are telling her about the "God of the impossible."

While she's waiting for her clinic appointment, Ailce rebels: "I want to know what's going on. I don't see any improvement. When they do those heart surgeries, where they have to attach one nerve to another, they manage to fix things. Why don't they tie up what's inside me?" Ailce has forgotten not only what the doctors had explained long ago; she's also forgotten what she told me two months earlier. For the first time, I step in: "At this appointment, tell them everything you're feeling. Get all of your questions answered."

The doctor hugs Ailce tenderly. The sun shines through the window and seems to connect the two women seated across from each other, illuminated as if on stage. Ailce says: "I don't know what I've got." Dr. Maria Goretti Maciel replies: "Don't you remember our first talk?" Ailce doesn't. "I told you there was a stone in the middle of the road," the doctor says, quoting the poet Carlos Drummond de Andrade. Ailce hears the explanation again—and again her eyes follow the doctor's hand sketching out the architecture of death inside her. "But can't you jump over here and put it together?" Dr. Maciel says: "No, unfortunately we can't make a viaduct." This time Ailce presses on: "So there's no cure? So this will go on until . . ." And she cuts her sentence short.

The doctor's cell phone rings. The ringtone is the theme song from *Mission Impossible*. She hangs up.

"Everyone's life comes to an end one day. Yours, mine," the doctor says. "*Palliative* comes from the Latin word *pallium*, which means cloak. That's what we do here. We throw a cloak over the disease. The tumor releases toxins into the body, and this triggers symptoms. The drugs stimulate the appetite, alleviate the nausea, lessen the anxiety. But one day we won't be able to ease the symptoms anymore. When that day comes, my commitment to you is to never abandon you. We're going to take care of you until the end."

Ailce leaves the doctor's office standing tall, eyes dry. She's in heels. Her foot fails her, and she stumbles. For the first time, she takes my arm for support. But she is still herself: "Do you suppose if I put on a little weight, then they could do the surgery?" For the first time, I give myself permission to speak: "I heard everything the doctor said. It doesn't matter if you're fat or thin. It never mattered. It's not your fault. It's the tumor that's in a spot where it can't be removed." She looks at me sideways and says: "I think they'd already told me. But you can't remember everything."

By July, Ailce no longer gets out of bed or even opens the window. Plunged into a darkness that doesn't depend on the earth's rotation, she prefers to leave the sun outside. She wears diapers because she can't make it to the bathroom, feels cold even when it's hot. But she still tells stories and doesn't let me leave her house without a second helping of cake. "The past makes us live, don't you know?"

On Monday, July 14, her room holds the smell of death, and her body seems smaller on the bed. "My time is running out," she says. I know it's true because she has stopped fighting. The anger in her expires and her voice softens. When Ailce drinks water, still holding the cup in her own hands, she complains that it tastes bitter. She has always feared the pain, and the pain has arrived. "I'm tied up inside. I smell something rotten."

Ailce describes all the deaths in her family: her father, who died at home; her mother, in the hospital; her husband, of Chagas disease; her brother, in an accident. After this inventory of endings, she concludes: "Now it's me who has come to the very end."

The pain gets worse at night. Ailce asks her daughter to call Preto Velho, a spirit guide known by many names in Afro-Brazilian religions. When the entity manifests himself through Luciane's mouth, Ailce pleads: "Take me. Nothing else ties me to this world." Preto Velho jokes with her. "It's not that easy, my daughter. There's a line in heaven. I'm going to see if I can get you an opening so you can take care of kids." As part of this mystical contract, Preto Velho promises Ailce that he'll take her before the week is up. In a private conversation, he explains to the family: "It's spread all over. She feels like she's got thorns inside."

I've thought hard about how to describe this night. I came to the conclusion that the death is hers. Ailce has faith, and it's very ecumenical. Ever since she first fell ill, she never refused spiritual help. Every week she has taken communion from Catholic volunteers and she's never failed to open her door to priest or pastor. But it is the one she calls Preto Velho who comforts her during the longest night of her life. "I'm going, but I'll be back," he says. "I'm going to be with you, hold your hand. And I'm going to prepare a path of lilies for you to pass over. We're both old. I'll lend you my cane and stool. When I get tired, you get up and I'll sit down. When you get tired, I get up and you sit. You're not sick, your body is. Your soul is clean. And you are a flower."

The next morning, Ailce leaves her home for the last time, and for the very last time descends the stairs. She is carried down because she has no strength, her feet are bare and no longer touch the ground. Lourdes sobs and promises to shut the door tight. The parrot hasn't eaten for days. The dog, Dunga, whimpers and hides in his doghouse when he sees her go by. At the farewell of the woman who inhabited it, the house itself seems to be in its death throes.

In the hospital bed in the palliative care unit, Ailce asks me to pull off her socks. "I don't like feeling trapped," she explains. She is dying and her toenails are painted pink. Then she asks: "I think the story you're writing about me is coming to an end. What do you think?" I am cowardly: "I don't know." Her yellow eyes bore into me. "You don't know?" I lie. "I don't think there's anything missing." We both know death is missing.

I need to say: "And it's a beautiful life." She asks for confirmation: "Do you think so, Eliane?" I assure her: "You've always fought for what you wanted, raised your kids, built the house you dreamed of, satisfied the hunger of so many children. You've lived." And she concludes, so I won't forget: "I did it all without ever asking anyone for anything."

The drugs take effect and she slides into a serene sleep. Dr. Veruska Hatanaka works to keep her from feeling pain yet able to say goodbye to her family. It's delicate chemical engineering. Luciane has a fever of 104 degrees and feels every one of her mother's pains. Marcos brings his wife in to make peace with her mother-in-law. Ailce tries to smile and asks about her only grandchild, six-year-old Ramom. She wakes occasionally to ask for water, and insists on holding the glass. "The water is sweeter now," she says. Ailce is no longer hungry and this doesn't pain her anymore. But when she opens her eyes late that night, she asks if I've eaten.

On Wednesday and Thursday, Ailce just sleeps. Her brothers, neighbors, and friends take turns around her bed. They tell stories about her life. Her baby brother puts his big hand on her face, a worker's hand, and he cries. "I love you so much. What do you want me to do for you? Do you want some coffee, want me to bring you a coffee?" She opens her eyes, recognizes him, and mumbles: "I love you too." And she falls back to sleep. "We used to sleep in the same foldout cot, in the kitchen," says a girlfriend. "I was dating a guy who was the spitting image of Elvis Presley, and she was dating Maurício, a green-eyed blond." She laughs and cries. "My dad was madly in love with her," says Luciane.

A photograph of this moment shows Ailce in bed and her family around her. It looks like reality theater. There is movement in each of them, none in her. They talk about her, but she's not there. Ailce is exiting the stage, and the lives of everyone there will go on without her. Fragments of existence flutter about her in the form of memories as she dies. But Ailce still hears. She opens her eyes whenever someone pronounces her grandson's name. When we're alone, I say: "Thank you so much for telling me your story. I'm going to write a beautiful article about you. And I will never, ever forget you." I realize then that no one has ever trusted me so much. In many moments, I was the only witness to her life. I would write, and she would be dead. Ailce trusted me to write a story she would never read.

On Friday, July 18, Ailce wakes up after her bath. She is restless. It is hard to understand what she says. She asks for water, but now a piece of gauze has to be moistened and placed between her lips. She suffers, tosses in bed, and nobody knows where she finds the strength to contort her ravaged body. Nothing moves in the drains anymore. Ailce starts tearing off her clothes. She ends up naked. Late in the morning, Dr. Juliana Monteiro de Barros liberates her from the synthetic threads of her life. Ailce is free at last.

When her children arrive, Ailce recognizes them. She has been waiting for them. Then she falls asleep again. At three fifteen in the afternoon, she suddenly opens her eyes. She is lucid. While her mother's eyes wander the room, Luciane says: "Let's dance, Mom. Let's put on our clothes to dance. You're dressed like a gypsy and you look beautiful. You've been healed. There's nothing inside you anymore. Don't be afraid, I'm holding your hand. I'm going to help you cross over. Everyone is waiting for you. I love you so much, Mom. Thank you for everything."

Her daughter traces the outline of her mother's body with white petals. Ailce has a look of infinite sadness in her eyes. Her eyes roam the room and fix on the camera. And slowly her breath fades away.

ACKNOWLEDGMENTS

I owe many thanks for this book. First, everyone who opened the doors of their homes and lives to tell me their stories. This is a large gesture, and a risky one. Thank you.

The news story that brought me to Graywolf and Granta—"João Asks Raimunda to Die with Him in Sacrifice"—was first published in English translation in "Women Writing Brazil," a special issue of PEN America's *Glossolalia*, released in 2016. My deep gratitude to issue coeditors Eric Becker and Mirna Queiroz, who chose to include the piece. Raimunda and João's story speaks of dammed rivers but, paradoxically, it broke down barriers, impacting both their lives and mine.

The writer Diane Mehta, editor of *Glossolalia*, read me in English and suggested my voice was strong enough to break through the barrier of language and distances. With tremendous generosity, she drafted the project for this book. Graywolf believed in it, and Granta as well. The first joy the book gave me was this: discovering, at this gloomy time in the world, when words are used to create walls, that there are still editors who risk creating a book readers haven't asked for and don't even know they need.

I am grateful to the entire staff at Graywolf and Granta. Special thanks to Steve Woodward and Katie Dublinski, of Graywolf, and Ka Bradley and Laura Barber, of Granta, for the extraordinary commitment, respect, and professionalism they devoted so this book would materialize on bookshelves, within the reach of readers' hands and eyes. I have rarely seen such dedicated editors.

My immense gratitude to Diane Grosklaus Whitty, chosen to do the translation. She had already faced the pain and delight of transmuting into English the words of João and Raimunda, voices of a very singular Brazil, forged from earth, river, and searching, for the chapter that appeared in *Glossolalia*. There we discovered that our obsessions with words formed a possible intersection. We both know we fail, which makes us very attentive. If I had to be betrayed, since words don't convert but instead turn into others, I always trusted that Diane would be an honest traitor—and would betray me with tremendous talent. So I opened my body to her, because a translation doesn't happen unless the translator crosses the author's body and possesses it for some time. This isn't just any relationship. Diane and I became cohorts, betrayal became love. Sometimes I trust her more than I trust myself. And when she talks about my writing, I discover she knows more about me than I do.

Thanks as well to Michael Whitty, Diane's husband. For me, Michael became one of those people whom we've never met but have always loved. When Diane and I were plummeting into a word abyss, not knowing how to translate the untranslatable, I grew used to asking, "What does Michael think?" Since familiarity is a tricky thing, this eventually led to a certain impatience: "Where's that Michael?" Because with striking sensitivity, Michael always knew. For me, his word became the verdict. And he followed every day of this translation, sometimes startled, sometimes moved. For

Diane and me, Michael was the serene man during emergencies produced by insurrect words.

They were in the United States, I was in Brazil. They were in the capital of Wisconsin, I was in the wet, violent, and impassioned tropics of the Amazon. "I'll reply when I get back from the forest" was the brief message I often sent. Diane and Michael grew used to a routine that included rivers, jungles, indigenous and river people, and long periods without communication. And that's how we translated.

My thanks to Lilo Clareto, the photographer who has accompanied me since 2001, author of the cover photograph of the Graywolf edition and several of the photographs on the Granta cover. I am grateful for his partnership, loyalty, and talent.

My thanks to Raimunda Gomes da Silva, woman of the Xingu River, who agreed to be the face of this book. Through Raimunda, I learned to resist the world's violence without losing joy. Raimunda didn't give me just her story, she also taught me to laugh, if only out of insolence.

And my thanks to Jonathan Watts, whom I fell in love with while this book was being translated (and invented). Jon devoted many days of his vacation to reading the translation and offering the contribution of an extremely sharp eye for detail. A Londoner, he made his language a home for me. Beginning to love in English as well helped me open the boundaries of my body.

A book is a caring gesture on the part of many. There is much love in this book. My thanks for this. Always and always. And I hope this love on the part of so many, and my love for these stories so real they seem made up, has reached you.

TRANSLATOR'S NOTE

A journalist, says Eliane Brum, must learn to cross the street to the other side of herself if she is to hear the voice of the Other. And then make the trip back to share what she has learned, against the backdrop of our collective experience. Translators do something similar: they help their readers undertake a journey to the other side—to the depths of a forest, to the heartache of a cemetery, to a favela rooftop. Eliane says she never returns from her journeys the same, and hopefully the reader of a translation won't either, but will experience some shift, great or small, in the tectonic plates of his or her worldview.

In assisting readers on their trip, translators often try to smooth out the road, paving the way with familiar words and expressions, producing a text so "fluid" or "fluent" that "it might have been written in English." But if we are not to remain on the outside looking in, penetrating another culture requires us to move beyond familiar frames and lose our bearings a bit. This is especially true with Eliane, who shuns the commonplace and, like her subjects, "stretches the colonizer's language, poetizing the awesome." Eliane's is not the Portuguese language constrained by prescriptive grammarians or the Portuguese language used in official documents, which in its written form is imbued with the power to wreak destruction on the peoples of the forest, shape how we perceive the lives of residents of a favela, or rule on the fate of those condemned to death for devoting their lives to a factory.

There's an old joke about the difference between continental and Brazilian Portuguese, two versions of the same language that differ much as US and British English do: two Brazilians take a cab from the Lisbon airport to their hotel and spend the drive chatting away to each other. When they reach their destination, the cabbie turns around and asks, in Portuguese as thickly accented to the Brazilian ear as the English of some Irish speakers to an American: "What the devil language are you two speaking that I can understand every word but don't recognize it?!" I would like Eliane's English-speaking readers to have a similar wonder in their minds, as if another language were hovering somewhere beneath the surface, at times a little intriguing yet still fully comprehensible and very much their own. An impossible goal to meet, but one worth aiming at. And, after all, translation is an impossible act.

The most obvious way of reminding readers they have crossed a border is by leaving words in the original language, words so culture-bound that no exact equivalent exists. For example, "Adail Wants to Fly" gives readers a feel for Brazil's entrenched social hierarchies, reflected in this story in an apparently innocuous two-syllable word: *doutor*, or doctor. Since the days of the Empire, any Brazilian holding a bachelor's degree has had the right to this honorific, while, as recently as the 2010 census, only 4.4 percent of Brazilians had graduated college. Along the way, the term morphed into a generic form of address applied by the humble to the mighty. While my decision to preserve *doutor* does not directly inform the reader of all this, the unfolding of Eliane's interview with Adail does suggest how the term reflects hierarchical social relations. Hopefully, the reader will have a certain feel for the Portuguese word by the story's end. (My decision was also a way of avoiding any US- or British-bound cultural associations that might be conjured up by a translation like *sir*.)

I offer another simple example where my translation choice hopes to keep the reader more firmly planted on Brazilian ground, even at the risk of some slight puzzlement. In the chapter "In Demon Zé's Brazil," Eliane writes that some prospectors have a "*labia de pagodeiro*," something like the gift of gab of a *pagode* singer. This might have been rendered as "sweet-talking as crooners," using two terms wholly familiar to English readers, but I opted instead for "sweet-talking as *pagode* singers." Even if readers are unfamiliar with Brazilian *pagode* music, preserving the word *pagode* (which has already merited its own Wikipedia entry) gives them the chance to learn something about how its performers may be perceived.

I find further justification in such choices because Eliane herself doesn't present a predigested reading experience. She challenges us to rethink the boundaries of words and ergo to rethink, period. Like Adail, who stops cold at the entrance to Salgado Filho airport, Eliane's readers are sometimes pulled up short by her new twists on old phrases, by the way she ignores syntactic and semantic constraints (Portuguese is admittedly more pliable in this regard). Describing a worker's shirt in "The Noise," she says that "*havia nela uma vontade de missa*"—literally, "there was in it a will/desire for [liturgical] mass." After rejecting various other possibilities, I had settled on "it had an air of church about it." I was pleased with the flow of the phrase . . . until, on my fifth or so revision of the text, I saw the "cliché factor." Anathema to Eliane. For whom a man is not short but of brief stature, for whom hope does not cling to the wind but clutches it, for whom an eagle can ride rather than fly over mountains. So back to the drawing board and eventually to the solution "an urge for church about it," my attempt to convey something of the enigmatic quality of Eliane's original, perhaps giving the reader pause to ponder.

Eliane's voice shares much with the voices of the people portrayed in her stories and with their idiosyncratic speech, for which she has utmost respect. In "Old Folks Home," she comments on "the poetic prose that seems to germinate in the very placentas of people from the Northeast." Eliane and all the people who tell their stories in this book afford proof positive that the dictionary doesn't own its words, nor do grammar books own syntax. In "João Asks Raimunda to Die with Him in Sacrifice," João suffers a bodily reaction to the loss of his home and his lifestyle. In prosaic English, his legs become paralyzed, or freeze up. But his Portuguese is not prosaic, so neither can his English be. Instead: "My nerves locked everything all up. Locked up so tight I couldn't walk. . . . It's not easy to get so angry that your body locks up." His wife, Raimunda, recounts the pain of losing their island to the Belo Monte dam: "I didn't live on the island. I lived from it, and it lived from me." In João's words: "From here on in, I only see darkness in my sight. . . . I stay here staring at the world, looking for myself. Who can answer this search for me?" No, technically speaking, a "search" doesn't get "answered," but after a hydroelectric project locked up João's body, how can I compound that by damming up his words?

There are other moments of strangeness in the text. In "Forest of Midwives," Eliane does not deliver a lesson in midwifery practices but instead transports readers directly into the midwife's universe, no coaching, no preparation. When readers are told that the midwife "pulls the mother's belly, righting the child," they are no doubt a bit lost. This is soon followed by the information that "for the midwife, it is her mission to wash, cook, and pull the woman's belly every morning and every afternoon so she will be healthy." Typical Eliane, pushing her readers to wonder, in both senses of the word: to stop and ask what is happening and to stand in awe of a world where pulling bellies is a regular practice. In the literature on Latin American midwifery, the term is usually rendered as "abdominal massage" or "massage." It seemed to me that this rendering would snap the mind shut, narrowing the reader's understanding to only a fraction of what the practice involves. Using "massage" would also fail to mimic the experience of the Lusophone reader: first perplexity over an apparently simple, ordinary word and then the discovery of its meaning over the course of the story.

Up to here, I've written about translation as an act of addition, about how it can allow readers access to places, people, and experiences that would otherwise remain locked inside a jumble of inscrutable phonemes. Now for the inevitable, and infamous, losses. First, the obvious: the beauty of Portuguese itself, its musicality and cadence, where rivers and oceans flow through its syllables. Gone. Slashed and burned. Also lost are the memories, the associations, the smells and sounds even one single word can evoke, in any language. Then there are the cultural allusions to a legacy shared across generations, genders, and classes of Brazilians, and yet still specific to each person's experiences. Sometimes this comes in the form of a musical sound track. In "A Country Called Brasilândia," as soon as Brazilian readers are told "More than sixty years ago, something happened where Avenida Ipiranga crosses Avenida São João," many automatically hear Caetano Veloso singing "Sampa." Eliane goes on to provide enough information to steer the reader to the famous song, but what is lost is the reflexive, unbidden sound of Caetano's velvet voice in the reader's head, of something that happens in the hearts of all of his fans as the chords take them back to a certain time in the history of Brazil and of their lives.

For me, the most painful losses occur at the level of Eliane's linguistic creativity. Her word choices are precise, never accidental, and like the people she has interviewed, her use of language is free-ranging. She will sometimes use a word to clearly convey "definition 1" from the dictionary, yet tucked inside comes "definition 2," along with a shadow of other sensations or interpretations. In "Burial of the Poor," a mother who has just interred her infant son is "keeping vigil over the health of her six-year-old daughter." "Keeping vigil" is my rendering of *velar*, a verb that links the act of protecting life with the act of burying it, because it means "to keep watch over," but also refers to an important rite in Brazilian society: standing at the side of a casket during a funeral visitation, which not infrequently requires a nightlong vigil. In Portuguese, even as we observe the mother protecting her daughter's health, we may feel the cemetery lurking in the background.

Eliane also combines verbs or expressions in novel ways. In "A Country Called Brasilândia," she tells us that most women in the community *se desvira*, a neologism that takes a common expression that means to cope with a situation resourcefully (*se virar*) and adds a prefix (*des-*) to create an unusual, reflexive use of another verb (*desvirar*), which in turn means to twist or turn something so that it goes back to its original position. Novel as this usage is in Portuguese, it is thoroughly comprehensible to the Brazilian reader, who immediately understands that these women are bottomless wells of resourcefulness. Perhaps a better solution will hit me in the early hours of some sleepless morning, but until then, I have admitted defeat with this simplification of Eliane's sleight of language: "most women . . . turn themselves outside in, doing a thousand and one things to pay the bills."

This was the compass I followed in my endeavor to transport Eliane Brum's voice to an English-reading audience. Her words have no doubt arrived here in this other culture showing some scuff marks and a bit of jet lag, but I hope I have done some justice to their beauty and challenges, and also to the voices of so many unseen Brazilians whose stories they tell, the heart of this book in any language.

I owe many thanks. To Diane Mehta, for envisioning this book and finding it a home in English. To Steve Woodward, Katie Dublinski, and the other staff at Graywolf, for entrusting the project to me and helping shape it into final form. To Ka Bradley, of *Granta*, for her thoughtful observations. And to the translation colleagues who generously lent me their ears, ideas, and words (Catherine Jagoe, Margie Franzen, Thais Passos, Ben Kearney, Bryon MacWilliams, Alison Entrekin), and other friends who also commented on chapters (Pat Henson, Rachelle Richardson, Caren Meghreblian, Harry Bernstein, Brian Chullino, Paul Fankhauser).

As ever, my daily gratitude to Michael, my husband and first reader, who now knows this book almost as thoroughly as I do. His insights, creative contributions, and loving support were invaluable.

Lastly, my deep thanks to Eliane, first for being the reporter, and person, she is, turning "unhappenings" into events demanding of the world's attention. Second, for the privilege of inhabiting her body of language and attempting to transport it across cultures. It was for this book that I became a translator.

—*Diane Grosklaus Whitty*

PUBLICATION ACKNOWLEDGMENTS

The essays in this collection have previously appeared in the following publications:

"Forest of Midwives" – *Época*, March 27, 2000.

"Burial of the Poor" – *Zero Hora*, June 6, 1999. This translation first appeared in *Becoming Brazil: New Fiction, Poetry, and Memoir* in *Mānoa: A Pacific Journal of International Writing* 30, no. 2, (Winter 2018), pp. 36–38.

"Crazy" – *Zero Hora*, September 4, 1999.

"The Noise" – *O Verso dos Trabalhadores*, Editora Terceiro Nome, 2015.

"A Country Called Brasilândia" – *Época*, February 12, 2007.

"Eva against the Deformed Souls" – *Zero Hora*, August 14, 1999.

"In Demon Zé's Brazil" – *Época*, February 5, 2007.

"Adail Wants to Fly" – *Zero Hora*, June 12, 1999.

"The Man Who Eats Glass" – *Zero Hora*, February 6, 1999.

"Old Folks Home" – *Época*, December 24, 2001.

"The Collector of Leftover Souls" – *Zero Hora*, May 29, 1999.

"Living Mothers of a Dead Generation" – *Época*, July 31, 2006.

"The Middle People" – *Época*, October 4, 2004.

"The Voice" – *Zero Hora*, November 27, 1999.

"João Asks Raimunda to Die with Him in Sacrifice" – *El País*, September 22, 2015. This translation first appeared in "Women Writing Brazil: A PEN American Publication," *Glossolalia* no. 2, (Fall 2016), pp. 15–37.

"Captivity" – *Zero Hora*, September 11, 1999.

"The Woman Who Nourished" – *Época*, August 18, 2008.

"Forest of Midwives," "A Country Called Brasilândia," "In Demon Zé's Brazil," "Old Folks Home," "Living Mothers of a Dead Generation," "The Middle People," and "The Woman Who Nourished" also appeared in *O Olha da Rua* (Porto Alegre, Brazil: Arquipélago Editorial, 2008; second edition, 2017). "Burial of the Poor," "Crazy," "Eva against the Deformed Souls," "Adail Wants to Fly," "The Man Who Eats Glass," "The Collector of Leftover Souls," "The Voice," and "Captivity" also appeared in *A Vida que Ninguém Vê* (Porto Alegre, Brazil: Arquipélago Editorial, 2006).

ELIANE BRUM is a Brazilian writer, journalist, and documentary film-maker. She has received more than forty awards and honors at home and abroad, including the Vladimir Herzog, Inter American Press Association, and King of Spain prizes, making her Brazil's most award-winning journalist. In 2008, she received the United Nations Special Press Trophy "for everything she has done and is doing in defense of justice and democracy." She spent eleven years as a re-porter for the newspaper *Zero Hora*, in Porto Alegre, and ten years for the magazine *Época*, in São Paulo. Since 2010, she has worked as an independent journalist and has developed long-term projects with the peoples of the Amazon forest and the "new middle class" on the outskirts of São Paulo. She has published five nonfiction books: *Coluna Prestes, o avesso da lenda* (1994, Azorean Prize for new au-thor), *A Vida que Ninguém Vê* (2007, Jabuti Prize), *O Olho da Rua* (2008), *A Menina Quebrada* (2013, Azores Prize for best book), and *Meus desacontecimentos* (2014). In 2011, she published the novel *Uma Duas* (shortlisted for the São Paulo Literature and Portugal Telecom Literature prizes), which was translated into English as *One Two* (Amazon Crossing, 2014). She has written and directed four documentaries: *Uma história severina* (2005, winner of seven-teen prizes), *Gretchen Filme Estrada* (2010), *Laerte-se* (2017), and *Eu+1—uma jornada de saúde mental na Amazônia* (2017). She cur-rently writes regular columns for *El País*-Spain, *El País*-Brazil, and *El País*-America. She is also a contributor to the *Guardian* and other European newspapers. She lives between Altamira, in the Amazon forest, and São Paulo.

DIANE GROSKLAUS WHITTY specializes in nonfiction in the fields of the social sciences, history, and public health. Her major book translations include *Activist Biology* by Regina Horta Duarte, *The Sanitation of Brazil* by Gilberto Hochman, and *Zika: From the Brazilian Backlands to Global Threat* by Debora Diniz. She has also translated prose and poetry by Adriana Lisboa, Marina Colasanti, and Mário Quintana, among others. Her translations have appeared in the *Guardian*, the *Lancet, History Today*, and *Litro*. She spent twenty-three years in Brazil but now lives in Madison, Wisconsin, with her husband.